南越国—南汉国
宫署遗址与海上丝绸之路

The Palace Site of Nanyue and Nanhan States
and the Maritime Silk Road

南越王宫博物馆　编著

Edited by Archaeological Site Museum of Nanyue Palace

文物出版社

Cultural Relics Press

图书在版编目（ＣＩＰ）数据

南越国—南汉国宫署遗址与海上丝绸之路 / 南越王宫博物馆编著 . -- 北京 : 文物出版社, 2020.4
ISBN 978-7-5010-6257-7

Ⅰ . ①南… Ⅱ . ①南… Ⅲ . ①南越（古族名）- 宫殿遗址 - 考古发现 - 广州 - 西汉时代 ②宫殿遗址 - 考古发现 - 广州 - 南汉 ③海上运输 - 丝绸之路 - 考古发现 - 广州 - 西汉时代Ⅳ . ① K878.34 ② K872.651

中国版本图书馆 CIP 数据核字（2019）第 188258 号

国家自然资源部地图审图号：GS（2020）2158 号

南越国—南汉国宫署遗址与海上丝绸之路

编　著　南越王宫博物馆

责任印制　陈　杰
责任编辑　黄　曲
责任校对　陈　婧

出版发行　文物出版社
社　　址　北京东直门内北小街 2 号楼
邮　　编　100007
网　　址　http://www.wenwu.com
邮　　箱　web@wenwu.com
经　　销　新华书店
制版印刷　北京雅昌艺术印刷有限公司
开　　本　787 毫米 ×1092 毫米　1/16
印　　张　11
版　　次　2020 年 4 月第 1 版
印　　次　2020 年 4 月第 1 次印刷
书　　号　ISBN 978 - 7 - 5010 - 6257 - 7
定　　价　198.00 元

《南越国—南汉国宫署遗址与海上丝绸之路》

编委会

主编：全 洪 李灶新

编委：李 郁 温敬伟 王雪静

编务：潘 洁

摄影：袁春霞 江松东

拓本：黎振安

展览工作人员名单

总 策 划：全 洪

项目负责人：李灶新 李 郁

项目组成员：胡 建 温敬伟 王雪静 潘 洁
　　　　　　石蕴慈 范彬彬 谭 文 姚基南

提 纲 编 写：潘 洁

形 式 设 计：王雪静

摄　　　影：袁春霞 江松东

拓　　　本：黎振安

The Palace Site of Nanyue and Nanhan States and the Maritime Silk Road

Editorial Board

Chief editor: Quan Hong, Li Zaoxin

Editorial board member: Li Yu, Wen Jingwei, Wang Xuejing

Editorial staff: Pan Jie

Photographer: Yuan Chunxia, Jiang Songdong

Rubbing Maker: Li Zhen'an

Exhibition Staff List

Chief planner: Quan Hong

Project leader: Li Zaoxin, Li Yu

Project member: Hu Jian, Wen Jingwei, Wang Xuejing, Pan Jie,
 Shi Yunci, Fan Binbin, Tan Wen, Yao Jinan

Outline Writer: Pan Jie

Form Designer: Wang Xuejing

Photographer: Yuan Chunxia, Jiang Songdong

Rubbing Maker: Li Zhen'an

目 录　CONTENTS

因水而生　因海而兴

——《南越国—南汉国宫署遗址与海上丝绸之路》代序

公元前 5 世纪以来，古希腊、波斯、印度和中国在政治和经济发展达到新高度，对世界的认知获得前所未有的成果。亚历山大东征给东方政治、经济、宗教、文化艺术带来冲击，也促进了中国与西方的经济贸易和文化交流。秦汉建立起强大的中央集权国家，通过西域及北方草原地带与中亚地区开展更多的经济、文化交往。汉武帝派遣张骞出使西域，从此凿空中国与西方交流的官方通道，是丝绸之路形成的标志性事件。与此同时，海上交通贸易也发展起来，汉朝政府派出使节到达印度洋。海上丝绸之路通过各港口城市建立国际贸易网，将各国联系起来。学界把海上丝绸之路的发展分为五个历史阶段：秦汉时期为形成期，三国晋南朝时期是发展期，隋唐时期是繁盛期，宋元时期达到鼎盛，明清时期由盛转衰。

当前海上丝绸之路研究的内涵丰富，包括政治、外交、军事、商业、宗教、文化、科技、艺术、建筑、手工业等涉及当时人们物质生活和精神生活的方方面面，统括可分为民间和官方两种行为。这里侧重于官方行为，即各朝代政府的外交和对外贸易管理。

广州古称番禺，背靠越秀山—白云山，扼珠江出海口。《汉书·地理志》载其"处近海，多犀、象、毒冒、珠玑、银、铜、果、布之凑，中国往商贾者多取富焉。番禺，其一都会也。"是南海海上丝绸之路的发祥地。文献记载与自 20 世纪 50 年代以来的考古发现均表明，广州这个南方大港从汉代直到现在，上下两千年历久不衰。广州地区考古发现了众多与南海海上丝绸之路相关的遗迹和遗物。1995 年以来，我们在南越国宫署遗址发掘出公元前 3 世纪至公元前 2 世纪南越国和公元 10 世纪南汉国的宫殿、池苑遗迹以及历代官署遗迹，出土了一批具有东南亚、南亚和西亚等海外文化因素的遗物，确证遗址所在地既是两千年来岭南地区政治中枢，也是海上交通贸易管理中心。

从考古学文化遗存的角度阐述两千多年来海上丝绸之路发生、发展过程的研究成果已在"南越国—南汉国宫署遗址与海上丝绸之路"专题展览和本图册中体现，于此不再赘言。下面谨就海上丝绸之路史迹申遗工作、本次展览设想、编写提纲时遇到的问题，以及对一些史料的解读和重新认识等内容略作补充，不揣简陋，以期就教于方家。

—

因海上丝绸之路遗迹、遗物延续时间长，所处位置分散，文化遗存具有多样性。又因历经千年来的自然与人为破坏，许多重要历史遗迹多已湮没，遗物也难得保存，为将广州现存的海上丝绸之路文化遗产资源整合，深入研究，推进海上丝绸之路文化遗产申报世界文化遗产工作，同时推动遗产的保护、利用与持续发展，2007 年中共广州市委宣传部、广州市文化局组织广州市文博系统专业人员对地上、地下文物和文献资料进行全面调查，系统搜集资料并进行相关研究，编撰了三卷本的《海上丝绸之路·广州文化遗产》（2008 年文物出版社出版）。

2012 年 11 月 17 日，国家文物局在北京召开全国世界文化遗产工作会议，公布了更新的《中国世界文化遗产预备名单》。45 项文化遗产中，广州市的南越文王墓、南越国—南汉国宫署遗址、南海神庙及码头遗址、怀圣寺光塔、清真先贤古墓和光孝寺等 6 处史迹点列入。2016 年 4 月，国家文物局和国家海上丝绸之路申遗项目组对广州市海上丝绸之路申遗预备名单中的史迹点开展价值、真实性、完整性和保护管理现状现场调查和评估，明确了南越国—南汉国宫署遗址等 6 处史迹点入选"海上丝绸之路·中国史迹"首批申遗遗产点名单。

2016 年 5 月 11 日，广州市政府成立海上丝绸之路史迹保护和申报世界文化遗产工作领导小组，由市长温国辉任组长，副市长王东任副组长。领导小组下设办公室，王东副市长为主任。同时召开第一次海上丝绸之路申遗工作领导小组工作会议。印发《广州海上丝绸之路史迹保护和申报世界文化遗产实施方案》，对广州市海上丝绸之路申遗工作进行全面部署。2017 年 4 月 20 日，国家文物局在广州召开海上丝绸之路保护和申遗工作会议，通过了广州为申遗工作牵头城市的决议。2017 年，广州市对 6 处海上丝绸之路史迹点共 13 个文物单位进行了本体修缮、遗址展示和环境整治，并对其文化遗产价值进行深入研究，进一步突出和证实广州市海上丝绸之路申遗史迹点与海上丝绸之路的直接联系。

在编写海上丝绸之路申遗文本的同时，为配合政府部门申报海上丝绸之路世界文化遗产工作，扩大其影响，加大宣传力度，广州市海丝申遗办在各个史迹点设立了海上丝绸之路专题展览，进一步扩大海上丝绸之路价值及意义，充分挖掘各史迹点所承载的"海上丝绸之路"历史价值和人物故事，阐释史迹点与海上丝绸之路的关系，并举办包括学术研讨、公共讲座、巡回展览等系列活动。自 2015 年以来，南越王宫博物馆先后举办了"扬帆启航——中外古代海船图片展""梯航万里——南海海上丝绸之路图片展""海阔羊城——广州与海上丝绸之路图片展"和"辽阔的南海——广州与海上丝绸之路图片展"等，在此基础上举办"南越国—南汉国宫署遗址与海上丝绸之路专题陈列展"。这些展览在广东省的许多县市博物馆展出，还赴山西、江西、云南、河南、辽宁、香港等地甚至跨出国门远赴塞浦路斯展出。在巡展中不断检验和修改，并随着研究的深入和材料的积累，展览从内容到形式都有较大提升，从南越国—南汉国宫署遗址一个申遗点扩展到广州六处史迹，进而扩充到涵括广州两千年来海上对外贸易交通的历史，成为实物与图文相结合的专题陈列。将来有条件的话，还应将展览内容及研究范围扩大到岭南地区，虽然文献与文物留存多寡不一，但各地在不同时期、不同地段发挥着各自的作用，共同构筑一幅更加完整的历史画卷。如广西合浦、贵港和广东徐闻等地汉墓出土的海外珠玑、金银、玻璃器；广东遂溪、英德、肇庆出土的晋南朝玻璃碗、金银器、波斯银币以及各地发现的唐宋外销瓷等。除了岭南地区出土的域外遗物，我们还应该将视野投到海外发现的中国输出文物上，进而更全面深入地研究中西交通贸易所带来的文化交流。还应与国内外文博机构通力合作，举办形式多样、内容丰富的展览。

2017 年"5.18"国际博物馆日，由广州市海上丝绸之路申遗办主办、南越王宫博物馆承办的"南越国—南汉国宫署遗址与海上丝绸之路专题陈列展"在南越王宫博物馆开幕。专题展览突出展示南越国宫署遗址是广州两千多年来岭南地区政治、经济、文化中心和海上贸易管理机构所在地，是中国海上丝绸之路兴起、发展和繁荣历史变迁的重要历史见证。中国社会科学院学部委员、中国社会科学院考古研究所研究员、原所长刘庆柱先生应邀出席开幕式并致辞，还作了题为"'海上丝绸之路'起点与特点"的学术讲座。

在策划和筹备展览过程中，得到各方领导的关怀与支持，专家的指导与帮助。王东副市长毕业于清华大学建筑系，是教授级高级建筑师和国家一级注册建筑师，对南越国宫署遗址出土的历代建筑构件十分感兴趣，自 2013 年以来常常介绍来穗的国内外建筑专家到南越王宫博物馆参观，并多次陪同。当我们介绍南越宫苑石筑及构件的来源可能与海外文化交流有关时，王副市长提出质疑，归纳为几点：一，来自西方，不能太过笼统，应该考证其来源；二，如果与西方有交流，在当时的背景下有无这个条件；三，中原地区无石材建筑，其不来源于中原文化，但有没有可能是越人自己的特点，或是在本土越式建筑基础上发生、发展呢？还指出不能光有推测，得有论证，找出证据，写成学术论文 [1]。

刘庆柱先生在参观展览后建议将展览周期延长至半年或以上，展览资料要及时整理出版，以供更多专家学者和读者研究探讨。广州市文化广电新闻出版局副局长欧彩群指示，南越王宫博物馆在做好海上丝绸之路遗址点申遗环境整治工作以外，可申请专项经费编辑出版展览图册。本书的编写与出版即渊源于此。

---

[1] 笔者于 2016 年前往印度考察，查阅文献，并对比同时期的各大文明的建筑特征，与李灶新合作撰写《南越宫苑遗址八角形石柱的海外文化因素考察》一文，发表于《文物》2019 年第 10 期。

二

　　举办展览是为了宣传，但宣传的基础是对文物和历史的深入研究。需要解决的学术问题首先是通过广州6个史迹点的历史及相关文物证实海上丝绸之路的价值；其次是各史迹点成为申遗点的依据及其符合标准的依据。由于这是申遗文本的任务，所以在展览中没有设置专门版面予以突出，但展览的内容一以贯之。

　　这次展览以实物、文字、地图、图片、年表等形式介绍了广州在海上丝绸之路的关键节点位置和地缘优势以及广州城市历史变迁，力求为观众提供对南越国宫署遗址——广州——海上丝绸之路层级、渐进的直观印象。该展览以南越国—南汉国宫署遗址为切入点，通过展示本遗址出土的与海上丝绸之路相关的文物，结合历史文献资料，介绍了广州自秦汉至明清时期不同阶段在"海上丝绸之路"的中心地位，最后对本遗址保护和海上丝绸之路申遗情况作了阶段性总结。

　　目前，广州虽然还没有发掘到可以确认的管理机构、港口、码头及仓储等方面的考古遗迹，但南越国宫署遗址是历代政府政令发布中枢所在。南越国时期出土舶来品，六朝时来往印度的高僧和来往南海及印度洋沿岸各国的商人和商船也多在广州登岸。唐代的史料丰富，中国史籍和阿拉伯游记都记录了广州是东方最大港口城市。五代十国南汉都城兴王府与海外诸国交通贸易，北宋在其基础上首设市舶司管理机构，使海外贸易管理专门化。虽然我们不能确指目前已发掘的房屋建筑究竟属于什么衙署，但政府机构应当就在这个遗址及其附近。因此，不论是南越宫殿、南汉宫殿、六朝基址，还是唐宋衙署、明清布政司，均是发布或执行政府对外交通贸易政令的地方，正是海上丝绸之路的见证。

　　本次展览重点是要突出中外交市的行政管理功能，改变以往侧重考古发现某个朝代某种器物的做法。广州（古称番禺）是南中国最早代表中央政府行使海上交通贸易管理港口的城市。公元前214年秦始皇统一岭南，设桂林、象、南海三郡，以番禺为南海郡治。秦始皇将岭南三郡首郡命名为南海郡，从台湾海峡到北部湾控制南中国海岸线，昭示着对海洋——南海开发经营的意志。

　　赵佗建立南越国，定都番禺。南越国在秦的技术和物质基础上利用漫长海岸线的独特优势，将番禺发展成为海外奇珍的集散地，同时汇集经西江、北江来自蜀地和岭北的货物，是当时全国十九个都会之一。虽无关于南越国海上交通贸易的文字记载，政府机构的行为不得而知，然则从出土文物可以看到商品贸易，工匠、艺术家、旅行者等人员的来往，经济与文化的交流等，域外奇珍、珠玑宝物以及制作形式和技术也随之输入中国。南越王墓出土的波斯银盒、红海乳香、金珠串饰、焊珠金花泡钉等海外珍异，如果说这些是舶来品的话，那么南越王宫池苑富有海外特色的石质构件则反映出南越工匠受到域外的设计样式启发，抽取印度建筑中部分元素并结合自己的习惯制作出南越宫苑园林建筑。八角形石柱出现于宫苑建筑，表明南越政权乐意接受这种新的建筑样式，是王室推动了海外交通活动的开展。凡此种种都反映出海上丝绸之路至少不晚于南越国时期就已经开辟，南越国宫署遗址就是最初、最好的见证。

汉武帝统一岭南，在南越国开辟南海交通的基础上，进一步拓展对外交通贸易，通过南海海域到中南半岛、马来群岛、南亚次大陆，经印度与西方世界交流，初步奠定了"海上丝绸之路"的基本航线。刘庆柱教授在讲座中提出：汉武帝时中国汉朝政府派出使节出使南海诸国，其意义足与张骞通西域相当，是官方海上丝绸之路发展的标志性事件。海上丝绸之路和国家的经济有关，和政治有关，和外交有关。汉武帝遣使南洋到印度洋，标志着汉朝海上政治外交的开始，是国家意志和实力的体现。

汉武帝置初郡十七，岭南九郡即以南海为首郡，因此南海郡治番禺县的官署自然就是执行中央政令、下达具体指示的行政机关所在。汉武帝的使者即皇宫侍郎，是中央的特派员，来到南海郡，必然首先安顿在郡治，由当时的郡守接待。郡守把使者送上船，就在番禺城的珠江岸边举行仪式。对于海上丝绸之路，番禺、合浦、徐闻、交州都有早期的港口，但是和政治关系最密切的是番禺。番禺才是海上丝绸之路的起点。

汉使者开通海上丝绸之路后，岭南地区西汉中期墓开始随葬大量具有海外特征的器物，典型的有各种材质组成的珠串饰、玻璃器皿以及胡人形象的托灯俑，一直延续到东汉末期，深刻地影响岭南民众日常生活习俗。更高端、珍稀的宝物可能经番禺辗转到京师及诸侯王国。

公元 3 世纪至 7 世纪的海上丝绸之路，除了传统以奇珍异宝为主的物质贸易，最突出的变化莫过于佛教东传。佛教文化从陆路和海路传入中国，六朝时来广州译经传教的僧人明显增多。法显法师亲赴印度，掀起了西行求法运动。他撰写的《佛国记》记录了印度至广州的航线，对中国航海事业产生深远影响。

六朝时西方与中国"舟舶继往，商使交属"，反映海上交通贸易发展的史料渐多。当时派驻广州的南海太守、广州刺史等政府官员代表朝廷管理海上交市。相对前后各历史时期而言，与海上丝绸之路有关的六朝遗迹、遗物发现得并不多。除了大量涌现的莲花纹瓦当反映出当时受印度文化影响的新风尚外，体现海陆两道与萨珊波斯密集交往的金银器、玻璃器和银币等却在广州鲜有出土，这应当与六朝实行的外商来华交市货易和管理方式有关。史书记载"外国贾人以通货易"，"海舶每岁数至"，最多也就"岁十余至"，证明一来数量不大，二来交市物品多为宝货、珍怪、异物，其中还有不少是动物、植物以及香料等。《梁书》卷五四《海南诸国》载梁武帝普通三年（522 年），婆利国（有研究认为其故地在加里曼丹岛北部，即今文莱）"其王频伽复遣使珠贝智贡白鹦鹉、青虫、兜鍪、琉璃器、吉贝、螺杯、杂香、药等数十种"。这些物品基本上集中在权贵手中，对民众生活没有带来多大影响，因此在墓葬和遗址里遗留较少。地方官员亦多私蓄方物，甚至私自将宝物带离广州，典型代表是西晋太康九年（288 年）司马奇"亦好畜聚，不知纪极，遣三部使到交广商货，为有司所奏"（《晋书》卷三十七《义阳王传》）。

另一方面，太守、刺史们要将收购的货物运输到天府，六朝都城建康（今南京）好多奇珍异宝都是由广州每年多次贡献而来（《南史》卷五十一《萧劢传》）。

　　唐代是中国海上交通史的新纪元。随着唐代中期经济重心向东南转移，加上阿拉伯帝国阿拔期王朝的兴起，在继承波斯与中国海上交通贸易传统的基础上，大食人进一步加强了与大唐的贸易。同时西域通道被吐蕃、突厥等阻隔，客观上促使南海海上丝绸之路达到新的高峰，商业上的利益与年俱增。

　　"市舶"与"市舶使"是两个不同的概念，从文献角度而言两者同时出现于唐代[2]。目前大多数研究集中于"市舶使"，发表了许多论文，但对"市舶"这种海上交市管理行为的研究其实更加重要。由广州地方行政长官（都督—节度使）及其僚属掌管市舶是南朝以来的传统。唐玄宗开元二年（714年）派遣市舶使参与市舶事宜。唐德宗朝市舶使由监军兼领，市舶使遂由原来的临时出使转变为相对固定的常驻职使。韦光闰《进岭南王馆市舶使院图表》对市舶使院建筑进行了简略的描述："近得海阳旧馆，前临广江，大槛飞轩，高明式叙，崇其栋宇，辨其名物，陆海珍藏，狥公忘私。"记载了利用海阳旧馆加以整修、建造市舶使院的史实，市舶使自此有了固定的办公地点[3]。但其所记地点在离宫署遗址发掘区域较远的珠江边。

　　文献中可检索的州事厅官衙名称除了市舶使院还有岭南飨军堂。在文豪柳宗元笔下的飨军堂则是另一处与海上丝绸之路有密切关系的建筑物，它在最高权力机关岭南道署的"都府"（都督府的简称）衙内，是招待外宾的重要场所。元和八年（813年）十二月，桂管观察使马总任广州刺史、岭南道节度使，为"增德以来远人，申威以修戎政，大飨宴合乐，从其丰盛"，重建飨军堂。次年，柳宗元应邀作《岭南节度飨军堂记》记载其盛况："先是为堂于治城西北陬"，"为堂南面，横八楹，纵十楹"，其范围之大、屋亭之多，令人惊叹，还增浚泉池，使人"如在林壑"，"弥望极顾，莫究其往"，节度使在新堂大摆宴席，"卉裳罽衣，胡夷蛮蛋，睢盱就列者，千人以上"，来自中亚的大夏、康居，南海的诃陵，东海的流球等多国使者和商人千人以上参加了此次礼成活动。

　　南越国宫署遗址发掘的唐代文化层有建筑基址、道路、水井等众多遗迹和遗物，房屋基址因缺乏文字资料而无法与都督府、节度使署的官衙对应。

　　唐代与海上丝绸之路有关的出土文物并不是以舶来物为主，而是重大历史产物——外销瓷。海船大容量的装载能力使陶瓷成为大宗出口商品。依前贤与今人的研究成果，唐代中期以来，"广州通海夷道"沿线——即从广州沿中南半岛、印尼群岛，经马六甲海峡到斯里兰卡、印度、波斯湾、

[2]　参见黎虎：《唐代的市舶使与市舶管理》，《历史研究》1998年第3期。
[3]　黄楼：《＜进岭南王馆市舶使院图表＞撰者及制作年代考—兼论唐代市舶使职掌及其演变等相关问题》，《中山大学学报（社会科学版）》2009年第2期。该文考证《进岭南王馆市舶使院图表》撰者为韦光闰，而非前人所说的王虔休。

阿拉伯半岛、东非——均发现众多中国陶瓷器，广州也出土众多同类器物，充分说明广州发挥着发舶港的作用。唐代广州是全国唯一派遣市舶使的城市，但南海交通贸易是否只能从广州放洋，目前还缺乏实证材料，尚不能做出判断。

学界关于海上交通贸易的研究多以唐宋为单元，这是因为唐宋时期为中国政治格局、政治制度更变的转型期（唐宋变革期），尤为重要的是实施了舶政，将海外交通贸易正式纳入法律的管理体系。但就管理体系而言，唐、宋差异较大。唐代前期依循南朝以地方行政官员为主的管理模式，中期后派遣市舶使和监军使参与市舶管理，创立新的管理方式。这种专务市舶管理的方法为宋所继承和发展。宋代首次订立市舶条例，被元代所承袭，前后相贯。

宋朝在广州最先设置海上贸易管理机构。开宝四年（971年）甫灭南汉即置市舶司，此时距赵宋建国已有十年，可以说是夺取广州之后才设立市舶司，是建立在唐、五代广州发达的海外贸易的基础上。宋市舶管理由唐遣使进步为置司，元丰三年（1080年）又修订《广州市舶条》。

宋朝海外贸易分官府经营和私商经营两种方式，大大改变了贸易种类和结构。宋元是民间海外贸易最兴盛的时期。宋太宗"雍熙中，遣内侍八人赉敕书金帛，分四路招致海南诸蕃"，鼓励"商人出海外蕃国贩易"。宋元时期中西志书和游记较前代更为丰富，可是出土的相关遗物则相对较少。自晚唐开始进口大量香料，并一改以往珠玑珍宝等奢侈品交市，而是外销大宗商品陶瓷器。宋元进一步发展，所以在考古发掘中反而较少发现珠玑、金银等舶来器物。与此同时，佛教也完成华化，印度佛教式微，来自海外的佛教文物也随之减少。宋代进出口货物达410种以上，按性质可分为宝物、布匹、香货、皮货、杂货、药材等，单是进口香料，其名色就不下百种。这些物品恰恰是考古发掘较少能发现的。

南越国宫署遗址宋代文化层发现大量国内各窑口瓷器，这无疑是从广州发舶的一个证明。同时也可以看到，北方窑口的器物相对比南方窑口的少，说明宋代外销器在不同的口岸发舶。时贤已经指出，因应海外市场的需求，外销瓷器绝非只供外销，大量本地生产的器物也供本地居民使用。遗址中生活基址、水井中发现的文物都足以说明。外来文化因素造型的瓷器也不仅供外销，同时又为国内民众所使用，增加了生活情趣，改变了审美观念。

说到广州为中国海上丝绸之路重要港口历两千多年不中断，最大的疑问莫过于泉州在南宋后期至元代初期在对外交通贸易中地位超越、取代广州的说法。

宋太祖开宝四年（971年）在广州设置的第一个市舶司（广南东路市舶司），一直运作到南宋末祥兴元年（1278年），前后三百余年。元祐二年（1087年）才在泉州增置福建路市舶司，至1276年南宋灭亡，近两百年。诸司均在广州市舶司后设置，形成以广州为首，泉、明、杭三州次之的格局。

泉州未设市舶司之前，泉州舶商出海贸易需到两浙或广东市舶司申请出海证明。"商人出海外蕃国贩易者，令并诣两浙市舶司请给官券，违者没入其宝货。""泉人贾海外者，往复必使东诣广，否则没其货。"元丰三年（1080 年），《广州市舶条》规定："诸非广州市舶司，辄发过南蕃纲舶船，非明州市舶司而发过日本高丽者，以违制论。"由此可见，宋代泉州海上交通贸易取得长足进步，但依然是在广州、宁波之后 [4]。

1974 年福建泉州后渚港发掘出南宋木船，船上发现一批包括香料等遗物在内的海上丝绸之路相关文物，考古文物与历史专家积极探讨泉州作为中国古代一大贸易港的历史地位。有学者提出："至少在南宋末年，泉州已经是江浙及福建通往海外进行贸易的主要门户。泉州港也逐渐有超过广州、成为居于首位的海外贸易港之势。""宋金战争和宋廷南迁，是泉州港在南宋时崛起的重要政治因素。"[5] 也有研究指出，到理宗绍定年间（1228~1233 年），泉州市舶贸易终因不景气而撤销专职提举市舶，改由泉州知州兼管。南宋末年，泉州市舶司在当地市舶贸易极度衰败之际被撤销。实际上，南宋后期，泉、广两地的市舶贸易都在走向衰败，泉州的衰落比较急剧，广州则要平缓得多 [6]。

从史料上看，泉州无疑是南宋与元代重要的对外贸易港口。南宋时，泉州因较广州更加靠近都城临安，其地位上升。到了元代，由于官本船等保护官员利益政策，航运大户利用近海和大运河的优势，多聚集于江南，使泉州获得强劲的发展势头。与泉州市舶司不同的是，广州发舶只向南海，泉州则是可经广州向南海或经明州向东洋。

元陈大震《大德南海志》卷七《舶货》载："广为蕃舶凑集之所，宝货丛聚，实为外府。……海人山兽之奇，龙珠犀贝之异，莫不充储于内府，畜玩于上林。"书中所载，从广州出洋涉及国家达 147 个，远逾前代。与泉州、庆元等港口将各种海外货物输往京城一样，从广州也有大量奇珍输送到内府。尽管宋元时期海上交通贸易的格局已经发生重大变化，对外的口岸更多，官民分头出洋，形式更多样，但并不影响广州作为通往南海的第一大港的地位。

明初在宁波、泉州和广州分别设置市舶提举司，指定宁波通日本，泉州通琉球，广州通占城、暹罗和西洋诸国。从各市舶司分管各国市舶的区域范围看，广州包揽了南洋至西洋的广阔区域。在明代，其他市舶司罢革时有发生，但广州市舶司却一直未曾关闭。朱元璋改变了前朝海外贸易自由的方针，实行闭关禁海的政策和备战的海防体制，颁令"禁濒海民不得私出海"，中国海商力量大受打击。郑和下西洋后，中国官方的船舶已不在印度洋出现了，但是民间出洋贸易势不可挡，在东南亚的市场上依然保持优势。

清康熙平定三藩之乱、统一台湾之后，解除明朝以来三百余年的海禁，实行开海通商政策。康熙二十四年（1685 年），正式设立"四大"海关：广州粤海关、厦门闽海关、宁波浙海关和

[4] 关于宋代市舶瓦器的内容，参见杨文新：《宋代市舶司研究》，厦门大学出版社，2013 年。
[5] 吴泰、陈高华：《宋元时期的海外贸易和泉州港的兴衰》，《海交史研究》1978 年第 1 期。
[6] 章深：《南宋市舶司初探》，《学术研究》1992 年第 5 期。

上海江海关。乾隆二十二年（1757年），英国商船队抵达浙江宁波口岸。宁波虽然设有海关，"向非洋船聚集之地"，而且宁波是海防要地，因此清政府认为不应让洋船在闽浙一带进出。乾隆颁旨："嗣后口岸定于广东，不得再赴浙省。"闽海关、浙海关、江海关停止中西贸易，欧美船只全部集中到粤海关。由此，"四口通商"变成了"一口通商"。这一政策一直延续到"鸦片战争"。在列强炮舰威逼下，在广州、厦门、福州、宁波、上海实施"五口通商"。

近百年的垄断进出口贸易，是广州港对外贸易最繁盛时期。粤海关成立之后，十三行正式建立。这是清政府重开海禁以来，特许经营对外贸易的十多家广州商行（还有"公行""洋行"等称谓，统称"十三行"）。道光二十三年（1843年），十三行全毁于一场大火。今天，人们只能通过十三行路上留传着的几个商行号名，回想当日的辉煌。

三

本次展览立足于阐述考古遗存与海上丝绸之路的关系，即关联性。南越国宫署遗址是公元前3世纪至公元前2世纪南越国、公元10世纪南汉国的王宫以及各朝代官署所在，政令出于殿堂，然而这是考古遗址和出土文物因缺乏文字记载所不能直接说明的。展览不能只是遗物的陈列，还应与文献及历史事件、历史人物相结合，从而讲述海上丝绸之路的形成与发展历程。其内容已不限于考古遗址本身，要扩展到更多方面，才能展示海交史的面貌，因此，吸收最新研究成果，加入虽不在广州出土、但与广州有密切关系的文物就很有必要。例如1989年陕西西安市西郊出土的三笏银铤，是波斯胡商伊娑郝的遗产，由广州官员进贡给唐德宗。其中一笏刻铭有使持节都督广州诸军事、广州刺史、充岭南节度副大使张伯仪和岭南监军、市舶使刘楚江，"体现了唐代海外贸易由岭南节度使和市舶使两套机构共同管理，管理海外蕃舶以岭南节帅为主，市舶使为辅"[7]。又如1984年在陕西泾阳县发现的《杨良瑶神道碑》，杨良瑶于唐德宗贞元初年从"南海附舶"出使黑衣大食，这是目前发现的唐王朝正式派遣使节航海下西洋的最早的确切记录[8]。

本展览还有一个突破是加入了对海外贸易管理有突出贡献的人物的介绍。依据历史记载挑选历代相关人物，根据重大事件为背景创作画像，从而更加形象、具体地向观众讲述历史人物的事迹及对海上丝绸之路发展的贡献。

南海道自秦汉以来就是中国对外交通贸易的海道，佛籍文献记录着丰富的海上丝绸之路史料，天竺译师从广州登岸进入中国传教的事情不绝于书。东晋法显是中国至印度的第一人，同

[7]　李锦绣：《从波斯胡伊娑郝银铤看唐代海外贸易管理》，《暨南史学》第八集，广西师范大学出版社，2013年。
[8]　张世民：《杨良瑶：中国最早航海下西洋的外交使节》，《咸阳师范学院学报》第20卷第3期，2005年。

时又是取海路回中国的第一人。初唐义净也是从广州赴印度取经的高僧。法显、义净均是早期海上丝绸之路的标志性人物。

市舶贸易管理政策实施在于人，以政府官员为代表的历史人物则侧重于其对海上交通贸易管理方面的作用，包括正、反两方面。人物的选取标准，是根据史书记载，在广州工作期间，对海上贸易管理方面的贡献能有传说或遗迹留传。如西晋吴隐之，是史籍记载与海上丝绸之路有直接关系的政府官员，他留下的贪泉诗句与史迹反映革除以前刺史皆多黩货之弊，拒绝"越岭丧清"的决心，对后世影响深远。唐代诗文但凡提及贪泉，也多数与海外珍物有关。

与蕃舶交市有关的清廉官员，早在宋代就已经为之立祠。《南海百咏·十贤祠》序云："在郡治之城上。前太守常以吴隐之、宋璟、李尚隐、卢奂、李勉、孔戣、卢钧、萧昉为八贤。蒋颖叔复以滕脩、王綝益之，为十贤祠，自作序赞，列名刻石。别有八贤祠，盖潘美、向敏中、余靖、魏瓘、邵晔、陈世卿、陈从易、张颉也，乃连帅周自强所立。"

本次选取的唐大历八年（773 年）任岭南节度使的路嗣恭则是一反面人物。路平定哥舒晃反叛立功，然平叛时杀戮海外商人，没收其资财百万贯据为己有，招唐代宗怨恨。在宰相元载家搜出路嗣恭贿赂的一个直径达一尺的外国玻璃盘，大小堪比法门寺地宫出土的琉璃盘。

需要说明的是，明清以降以中国丝绸、瓷器和茶叶为大宗的对外贸易商品大量随洋舶出口，西方的器具、手工技术、艺术作品等也随之传到中国，形成东西方交流的新格局。本次展览以考古出土资料为基础，加上广东省内各兄弟博物馆藏品丰富，曾举办多项此类专题展览，因此这部分内容涉及相对较少。

四

广州经考古发现的一批含有海外文化因素的遗迹、遗物以及历史遗留的古代建筑，包括宗教文化类的史迹，如佛寺、教堂以及一些墓地等，这些都是海上丝绸之路的物证，是我们认识和研究海上丝绸之路的重点。但是历代外商聚居地、活动场所以及最能直接反映海上丝绸之路的古代通商港口、码头迄今未有正式发掘，其地点及形制结构没能得到确认，这无疑是极大的缺憾。

还有不少学术问题未能解决，研究还不够深入。比如秦汉时期民间的交往已有诸多考古材料可鉴，然汉武帝之前秦与南越官方机构的外交行为还需要更多材料去论证。又如印尼水域发现的波斯船舶"黑石号"来华贸易的情形，关于其登岸及离港的港口城市就有广州说、扬州说。从唐代市舶发展的情势看，我们倾向于广州说，但缺乏对唐代港口城市的综合研究，尤其是对唐朝对外商船舶管理方式知之甚少。那时是否限定对外贸易口岸，如果有的话，又限定在哪些城市？

2007 年编写的三卷本《海上丝绸之路·广州文化遗产》只是资料汇编。麦英豪先生一再强调一定要善用这些材料，编撰《海上丝绸之路史》。这就需要广州文博界投入更多精力和人手，鼓励年轻人加入文物研究队伍，各单位亦要联合国内外学术研究机构和高等院校，共同努力把海上丝绸之路研究推上一个新台阶。

最后谈一谈笔者对广州海上丝绸之路申遗史迹命名的看法。目前申遗文本以"南越国—南汉国宫署遗址"作为申遗遗产点项目名称。这个名称突出了公元前 3 世纪至公元前 2 世纪和公元 10 世纪两个不同时期地方政权对海上贸易直接管理机构所在，但削弱了其他历史时期中央政府—地方官员以及特使管理的职能，并未能全面体现广州作为南海海上丝绸之路的东方最大港口城市的历史。广州的海上对外交通与贸易，自秦汉延续到现在，上下两千年，历久不衰，这在中国是独一无二的。

南越国宫署遗址是 20 世纪发掘时根据遗址性质确定的考古学命名，包括十二个朝代的地层堆积、历史遗存，是不同历史时期岭南地区政治文化中心和海上贸易管理机构所在，见证了广州港依托海上丝绸之路走向繁荣的历史。前面讲过的从未中断，说的就是这种行政管理职权的延续性。南越国宫署遗址是目前仅存的体现了各发展阶段的遗产点，通过出土实物与文献史料可以了解和认识海上丝绸之路在中国发展和演进的过程。然而，古代文物保存的形势不容乐观。广州作为岭南地区经济发展较快的中心城市，许多前代的与当代的史迹和遗物，随着城市更新换代的加快而日渐消失，加上经历两千年来的自然与人为的破坏，不少重要的历史遗迹都已湮没，目前仅有一小部分海上丝绸之路的文化史迹与遗物有幸留存。南越国宫署遗址的保护利用和展示就更显得弥足珍贵。因此，沿用考古学文化命名，以约定俗成的"南越国宫署遗址"作为申遗点名称，完全符合真实性标准，能更全面展示其与海上丝绸之路的关联性和长久性，更加符合申遗的第三条标准：或为一种已消逝的文明或文化传统提供一种独特的至少是特殊的见证。

南越王宫博物馆馆长：

Born from the River, Thrive on the Sea:

As the Preface of *The Palace Site of Nanyue and Nanhan States and the Maritime Silk Road*

Since the 5th century BC, the political and economic development of ancient Greece, Persia, India and China reached a new height, with the understanding of the world achieving unprecedented results. Alexandria's eastward expedition brought impact on politics, economy, religion, culture and art to the East, and meanwhile promoted the economic trade and cultural communication between China and the West. Qin and Han regimes established strong centralized empires, which carried out a lot of economic and cultural exchanges with Central Asia through the western region and the northern prairie region. The official communication channel between China and the West was built when Emperor Wu of the Han Dynasty sent Zhang Qian as an envoy to the western region, and this is also a landmark event of the formation of the Silk Road. At the same time, maritime transportation and trade also developed, as the Han government sent envoys to the Indian Ocean. The Maritime Silk Road linked various countries by establishing international trade network through port cities. The academic circle divides the development of the Maritime Silk Road into five historical stages: it is formed in Qin and Han Dynasties, developed in the Three Kingdoms Period, Jin and Southern Dynasties, prosperous in Sui and Tang Dynasties, reached peak in Song and Yuan Dynasties, and declined from prosperity in Ming and Qing Dynasties.

For now, research on the Maritime Silk Road is of rich connotation, including politics, diplomacy, military, commerce, religion, culture, science and technology, art, architecture, handicraft and other aspects related to people's material and spiritual life at that time, which all together can be divided into civil and official behaviors. This article mainly focuses on official behaviors, that is, the diplomacy and foreign trade administration of each dynasty.

Guangzhou, known as Panyu in ancient times, backs on Yuexiu and Baiyun mountains and faces the Pearl River estuary. According to *Han Shu· Di Li Zhi (Journal of Chinese Historical Geography in the History of the Han Dynasty)*, "it is located near the sea and there are many rhino horns, ivories hawkbills, pearls, silver and copper, as well as fruit and cloth, from which Chinese merchants gain much wealth. Panyu is one of the metropolises at that time." It is the birthplace of the South China Sea Maritime Silk Road. Both documents and archaeological discoveries since the 1950s show that Guangzhou has been prosperous for two thousand years from the Han Dynasty to the present as a great southern port. Many relics and remains related to the South China Sea Maritime Silk Road have been found in Guangzhou. Since 1995, we have excavated ruins of palaces, royal gardens and government offices of Nanyue state in the 3rd-2nd Century BC and of Nanhan state in the 10th Century AD from the palace site of Nanyue and Nanhan states, with a number of relics embodying overseas cultural factors such as Southeast Asia, South Asia and West Asia unearthed. It is confirmed that the site was not only the political center of Lingnan region for two thousand years, but also the administrative agency for maritime transportation and trade.

Research results demonstrating the emergence and development of the Maritime Silk Road over the past two thousand years from the perspective of archaeological culture are displayed both in the special exhibition and the catalogue of *The Palace Site of Nanyue and Nanhan States and the Maritime Silk Road*, which will not be further discussed. Hereinafter I would like to make some simple supplements to the application work of the Maritime Silk Road for the world heritage, the tentative plan of this exhibition, the problems encountered in the compilation of the outline, as well as the interpretation and re-understanding of some historical materials, and would like to listen to advices from the experts.

I

The relics and remains of the Maritime Silk Road are of long duration, scattered location and great diversity. Moreover, after thousands of years of natural and man-made destruction, many important historical remains have been annihilated, and relics are rarely preserved. In order to integrate the existing Maritime Silk Road cultural heritage resources in Guangzhou, conduct in-depth research, promote the application of the Maritime Silk Road for the world cultural heritage, and carry forward the preservation, utilization and sustainable development of the heritage, in 2007, the Publicity Department of Guangzhou Municipal Committee of the Communist Party of China, together with Guangzhou Municipal Bureau of Culture, organized professionals of relics and museology system in Guangzhou to conduct a comprehensive investigation of the over-ground and underground cultural relics as well as documents, with materials systematically collected and relevant research carried out, and three volumes of *The Maritime Silk Road · Guangzhou Cultural Heritage* (published by Cultural Relics Press in 2008) compiled.

On November 17, 2012, the State Bureau of Cultural Relics held a national working conference on national world cultural heritage in Beijing and released the updated preliminary list of world cultural heritage in China. Among the 45 cultural sites, 6 of Guangzhou were listed, including the tomb of King Wen of Nanyue state, the palace site of Nanyue and Nanhan states, the site of Nanhai temple and wharf, Guangta tower of Huaisheng temple, the tomb of Muslim sages, as well as Guangxiao temple. In April 2016, the State Bureau of Cultural Relics, together with national application project team of the Maritime Silk Road for the world cultural heritage, carried out field investigation and evaluation on the value, authenticity, integrity and preservation administration status of the historical sites of Guangzhou which were included in the preliminary application list of the Maritime Silk Road for the world cultural heritage, and made it clear that the 6 historical sites including the palace site of Nanyue and Nanhan states were selected into the first application list of the "Maritime Silk Road · Chinese Historical Sites" for the world cultural heritage.

On May 11, 2016, Guangzhou Municipal Government set up a leading group taking charge of the preservation work of historical sites and application work of the Maritime Silk Road for the world cultural heritage, with Mayor Wen Guohui as the group leader and deputy mayor Wang Dong as the deputy group leader. The leading group has an office, with deputy mayor Wang Dong as the director. At the same time, the first working conference of the leading group was held. The plan, which was for the implementation of the preservation of Guangzhou Maritime Silk Road historical sites and application of the sites for the world cultural heritage was printed, with the application work of the Maritime Silk Road for the world cultural heritage in Guangzhou comprehensively deployed. On April 20, 2017, the State Bureau of Cultural Relics held a working conference on the preservation of the Maritime Silk Road and the application for the world cultural heritage in Guangzhou, with the resolution of Guangzhou being the leading city in the application work passed. In 2017, Guangzhou carried out body repair, site display and environmental renovation at 13 cultural relics units in the 6 historical sites, and conducted in-depth research on their cultural heritage value, in order to further highlight and confirm the direct connection between the Maritime Silk Road historical sites of Guangzhou and the Maritime Silk Road.

While compiling the application text of the Maritime Silk Road for the world cultural heritage, in order to cooperate with the application work of the government to expand its influence and strengthen the publicity, several special exhibitions in each historical site of the Maritime Silk Road were held by Guangzhou Leading Group office of Conservation and World Heritage Nomination for Maritime Silk Road Heritage to further promote the value and significance of the Maritime Silk Road, fully excavate the historical value and character stories of the Maritime Silk Road carried by each site, and expound the relationship between the historical sites and the Maritime Silk Road, with a series of activities including academic seminars, public lectures and itinerant exhibitions held. Since 2015, Archaeological Site Museum of Nanyue Palace has successively held *Sailing: Photo Exhibition of Ancient Chinese and Foreign Ships, Sailing for Ten Thousand Miles: Photo Exhibition of the South China Sea Maritime Silk Road, Vast Sea in Yangcheng City: Photo Exhibition of Guangzhou and the Maritime Silk Road,* and *The Vast South China Sea: Photo Exhibition of Guangzhou and the Maritime Silk Road.* On this basis, the special exhibition of *The Palace Site of Nanyue and Nanhan States and the Maritime Silk Road* was held. These exhibitions were held in museums of many counties and cities in Guangdong Province, as well as in Shanxi, Jiangxi, Yunnan, Henan, Liaoning, Hong Kong and even abroad in Cyprus. During the tour, the exhibition was constantly inspected and modified, and with the research deepening and the materials accumulating, the exhibition was greatly improved from the content to the form, expanding from a single site to the 6 historical sites of the Maritime Silk Road in Guangzhou, and then covering the history of maritime foreign trade and transportation in Guangzhou for two thousand years, which finally became a special exhibition combining material objects with pictures and texts. In the future, if conditions permit, the exhibition content and research scope should also be expanded to Lingnan region. Although the extant documents and cultural relics of each place diverse a lot, they all play their own role in different periods and different areas to jointly build the complete historical picture. For example, overseas pearls, gold and silver, as well as glassware unearthed from the Han tombs in Hepu, Guigang of Guangxi and Xuwen of Guangdong, glass bowls, gold and silver wares, Persian silver coins of Jin and Southern Dynasties unearthed from Suixi, Yingde and Zhaoqing of Guangdong, along with porcelain for export of Tang and Song Dynasties, should all be taken into consideration. In addition to the foreign relics unearthed in Lingnan region, we should also take China's export cultural relics found abroad into account, so as to further study the cultural communication brought about by the transportation and trade between China and the West in a more comprehensive and in-depth way. It is also necessary to cooperate with domestic and foreign cultural institutions and museums to hold exhibitions with various forms and rich contents.

On May 18, 2017, the International Museum Day, sponsored by Guangzhou Leading Group office of Conservation and World Heritage Nomination for Maritime Silk Road Heritage and organized by Archaeological Site Museum of Nanyue Palace, the special exhibition of *The Palace Site of Nanyue and Nanhan States and the Maritime Silk Road* was opened in the museum. The special exhibition highlighted the palace site of Nanyue state as an important historical witness of Guangzhou being the political, economic, and cultural center of Lingnan region and the administrative agency of maritime trade for more than two thousand years, as well as the rise, development and prosperity of the Maritime Silk Road of China. Mr. Liu Qingzhu, academician of the Chinese Academy of Social Sciences, and researcher and former director of the Institute of Archaeology of the Chinese Academy of Social Sciences, was invited to attend the opening ceremony and addressed, with an academic lecture named *The Starting Point and Characteristics of the Maritime Silk Road* also given.

During the planning and preparation of the exhibition, we received care and support from all the leaders, as well as guidance and help from all the experts. Deputy mayor Wang Dong, graduated from the Department of Architecture of Tsinghua University, is a professor-level senior architect and national first-class registered architect. He is very interested in the construction of the architecture of the past dynasties unearthed from the palace site of Nanyue state. Since 2013, he often introduced domestic and foreign architectural experts who came to Guangzhou to visit the museum, and he himself also accompanied for many times. When we introduced that the origin of stone buildings and components in the royal garden of Nanyue state may be related to overseas cultural communication, deputy mayor Wang raised some questions which could be summarized as follows: first, the specific origin should be verified rather than too general as from the "West"; second, it should be identified whether there were suitable conditions to conduct communication with the West in the background at that time; third, there was no stone architecture in the Central Plains which meant they were not originated from the Central Plains culture, but whether there was possibility that they were characteristics of the Yue people themselves, or developed from the local Yue architecture should be further discussed. He also pointed out that there should be demonstration, evidence and then academic paper rather than mere speculation[1].

---

[1] In 2016, the author went to India to investigate, after which by searching documents and comparing architectural characteristics of contemporaneous civilizations, wrote a paper with Li Zaoxin called The Investigation of Overseas Cultural Elements Borne by Octagonal Stone Columns in the Royal Garden of Nanyue State was published in *Wenwu* 2019 (10).

After visiting the exhibition, Mr. Liu Qingzhu suggested that the exhibition period should be extended to half a year or more, with the exhibition materials arranged and published in time for more experts, scholars and readers to study and discuss. Ou Caiqun, deputy director of Guangzhou Municipal Bureau of Culture, Radio, Television, Press and Publication, instructed that the Archaeological Site Museum of Nanyue Palace could apply for special funds to edit and publish the exhibition catalogue in addition to the environmental renovation. This is where the origin of the compilation and publication of this book lies.

II

Though the exhibition is held for publicity, the foundation of publicity actually lies in the in-depth study of cultural relics and history. The academic problems need to be solved are: first, to confirm the value of the Maritime Silk Road through the history and related cultural relics of the 6 historical sites in Guangzhou; second, to find the basis on which these historical sites can apply for the world cultural heritage and facts that they can meet the application standards. As this is the task of the application text, there is no special layout in the exhibition, but the content of the exhibition is consistent.

This exhibition introduces the key node position and geographical advantages of Guangzhou on the Maritime Silk Road as well as the historical transformation of Guangzhou city in the form of material objects, texts, maps, photos and chronologies, striving to provide the audience with an intuitive impression of the gradual progress from the palace site of Nanyue state to Guangzhou, and then to the Maritime Silk Road. The exhibition takes the palace site of Nanyue state as the starting point, introduces the central position of Guangzhou on the Maritime Silk Road from Qin and Han Dynasties to Ming and Qing Dynasties by displaying the cultural relics related to the Maritime Silk Road unearthed from the site, and finally summarizes the preservation of the site and the application situation of the Maritime Silk Road for the world cultural heritage.

At present, although no identifiable archaeological remains such as administrative agencies, ports, wharves and warehouses have been found in Guangzhou, the palace site of Nanyue state was for sure the center for the issuance of government decrees. Many foreign products of the Nanyue state period were unearthed, while during the Six Dynasties many eminent monks from India as well as merchants and merchant vessels travelling on the South China Sea and in countries along the Indian Ocean docked in Guangzhou. There are rich historical materials of the Tang Dynasty, among which both Chinese historical records and Arabian travel records showed that Guangzhou was the largest port city in the East. In the Five Dynasties and Ten Kingdoms period, Xingwangfu, the capital city of Nanhan state, had trade connections with overseas countries, on the basis of which the Northern Song Dynasty firstly set up Bureau, making overseas trade administration specialized. Although we can't tell exactly what government offices the houses and buildings excavated are, the government agencies should be at the site and nearby. Therefore, whether the palace site of Nanyue and Nanhan states and the site of the Six Dynasties, or the government office of Tang and Song Dynasties and Bureau of Ming and Qing Dynasties, they were all agencies to issue or implement the government's foreign transportation and trade decrees, which all witnessed the development of the Maritime Silk Road.

The key point of this exhibition is to highlight the administrative functions in the communication between China and foreign countries, thus to change the previous practice of focusing on certain objects of certain dynasties found in archaeological discoveries. Guangzhou (formerly known as Panyu) was the first city of south China to exercise maritime transportation and trade administration on behalf of the central government. In 214 BC, Emperor Shi Huang of the Qin Dynasty brought Lingnan entirely under the control of the empire and set up Guilin, Xiang and Nanhai prefectures, with Panyu as the capital of Nanhai prefecture. Emperor Shi Huang named Nanhai prefecture as the leading one of the three Lingnan prefectures, controlling the coastline of south China from Taiwan Strait to Beibu Gulf, which showed his will to develop and manage the ocean - the South China Sea.

Zhao Tuo established Nanyue state and chose Panyu as the capital. By inheriting the basis of the technology and materials of the Qin Dynasty and taking the unique advantages of the long coastline, Panyu was developed by Nanyue into a distribution center for overseas treasures as well as goods from Shu and Lingbei regions coming in via Xijiang and Beijiang rivers, which was one of the 19 metropolises in China at that time. Although there is no written record on the maritime transportation and trade of Nanyue state and the behaviors of government offices were unknown, we can still see the trade of goods, the communication of craftsmen, artists and travelers, as well as economic and cultural exchanges and so on from the unearthed cultural relics, with foreign treasures, jewels, along with the production forms and technologies imported into China. The Persian silver boxes, Red Sea frankincense, stringed ornaments of gold beads, soak nails with welded beads and gold flowers and other overseas treasures were unearthed from the tomb of Nanyue king. If these are foreign products, then the stone components with overseas characteristics in the royal garden of Nanyue state can reflect that the craftsmen of Nanyue state were inspired by the design styles of foreign countries, and built the royal garden architecture by extracting some elements of Indian architecture and combining with their own habits. Octagonal stone columns appeared in the royal garden buildings, indicating that Nanyue regime was willing to accept this new architectural style, and the royal family promoted the development of overseas transportation activities. All of these reflect that the Maritime Silk Road had been opened up at least not later than the period of Nanyue state, and the palace site was the first and best witness.

Emperor Wu of the Han Dynasty brought Lingnan back under the control of the empire. On the basis of opening up the transportation of the South China Sea, he further expanded the foreign transportation and trade from the South China Sea to the Indo-China Peninsula, the Malay islands and the South Asian subcontinent, and started communication with the West through India, thus initially establishing the basic route of the Maritime Silk Road. Professor Liu Qingzhu pointed out in his lecture that during the reign of Emperor Wu, Chinese government sent envoys to countries in the South China Sea, the meaning of which was equivalent to Zhang Qian's access to the western regions, and was a landmark event in the development of the official Maritime Silk Road. The

Maritime Silk Road was related to the country's economy, politics and diplomacy. Emperor Wu of the Han Dynasty sent envoys to the Indian Ocean, and this marked the beginning of the Han Dynasty's maritime political diplomacy which also was the embodiment of national will and strength.

Emperor Wu of the Han Dynasty firstly set up 17 prefectures, and Lingnan prefecture was the leading one of the nine South China Sea prefectures. Therefore, the government office of Panyu county which was the capital of Nanhai prefecture was naturally the administrative agency that carried out the central decrees and issued specific instructions. The envoys of Emperor Wu, namely *Huang Gong Shi Lang* (servants of the royal palace), were special commissioners of the central government. When they came to Nanhai prefecture, they first settled down in the prefectural capital and were treated by the prefects at that time. When the prefects sent the envoy on board, the ceremony was held rightly on the bank of Pearl River in Panyu city. As for the Maritime Silk Road, although there were early ports in Panyu, Hepu, Xuwen and Jiaozhou, Panyu had the closest relationship with politics. Therefore, Panyu was the starting point of the Maritime Silk Road.

After the Maritime Silk Road was opened up by the Han envoys, a large number of objects with overseas characteristics started to be buried in tombs of the middle Western Han Dynasty in Lingnan region. Typical objects were stringed bead ornaments made of various materials, glassware, and figurines of foreign people's images holding the lantern, which continued to exist to the end of the Eastern Han Dynasty, profoundly affecting the daily life and customs of the people in Lingnan. More high-end and rare treasures may be transported to the capital and vassal states via Panyu.

In addition to the traditional material trade based on treasures, the most prominent change of the Maritime Silk Road during the 3rd to the 7th Century AD is the eastward spread of Buddhism. Buddhism culture was introduced into China both by land and sea. During the Six Dynasties, the number of monks who came to Guangzhou to translate scriptures and preach increased significantly. Master Fa Xian went to India in person and set off the movement of seeking Dharma in the West. *Fo Guo Ji (Biography of Buddhism)* written by him recorded the route from India to Guangzhou, which had a profound impact on the navigation industry of China.

During the Six Dynasties, the West and China had many exchanges via merchants and envoys while vessels came and went frequently, and there were more and more historical materials reflecting the development of maritime transportation and trade. At that time, the government officials, such as Nanhai *Tai Shou* (prefects) and Guangzhou *Ci Shi* (governors) dispatched to Guangzhou, administrated the maritime transportation on behalf of the imperial court. Compared with historical periods before and after, remains of the Six Dynasties related to the Maritime Silk Road were of a relatively small number. Apart from a large number of eaves tiles with lotus pattern reflecting the new trend influenced by Indian culture at that time, gold and silver wares, glassware and silver coins that can reflect the intensive communication with Sassan and Persia via land and sea were rarely unearthed in Guangzhou, which may be related to the trading goods and the administration of foreign trade in the Six Dynasties. Historical records said that foreign merchants bartered, and vessels came in only several times, ten times at the most, a year. Such records can prove that the number of goods was not large, let alone the goods for barter were mostly precious, rare and strange ones, including many animals, plants and spices. In Vol. 54 of *Liang Shu (History of the Liang Dynasty), Hai Nan Zhu Guo (States of the South China Sea)*, it is recorded that in the 3rd year of Putong period during the reign of Emperor Wu of the Liang Dynasty (522 AD), Pinjia, king of Poli (which is believed to be in the northern part of Kalimantan island, that is, present Brunei) sent envoys to China with dozens of treasures like white parrots, green insects, helmets, colored glazed wares, seashells, cups made of spiral shells, miscellaneous incense, medicine and so on. These items were mainly in the possession of powerful people, and had little impact on civil people's life, so they are rarely left in tombs and ruins. Local officials also stored and even took treasures away from Guangzhou without permission. Sima Qi can be the representative one, who was addicted to gathering treasures and had no limit. In the 9th year of Taikang period (288 AD) of the Western Jin Dynasty, he sent three envoys to Guangzhou to deliver goods, which was accused by government officials. [*Yi Yang Wang Zhuan (Biography of Yiyang King)*, Vol. 37 of *Jin Shu (The History of the Jin Dynasty)*]. On the other hand, chiefs and governors had to transport the purchased goods to the capital, and a huge number of the treasures in Jiankang (present Nanjing), the capital of the Six Dynasties, were tributes coming from Guangzhou for many times every year. [*Xiao Mai Zhuan (Biography of Xiao Mai)*, Vol. 51 of *Nan Shi (The History of the Southern Dynasties)*].

Tang Dynasty is a new era in the history of China's maritime transportation. With the economic center moving to the southeast in the middle Tang Dynasty and the rise of the Abbasid Dynasty of the Arab Empire, people of Dashi further strengthened their trade with the Tang Dynasty on the basis of inheriting the maritime transportation and trade tradition between Persia and China. At the same time, the western passage was blocked by Tubo, Tujue and so on, which objectively promoted the South China Sea Maritime Silk Road to reach a new peak, with commercial interests increasing yearly.

"*Shi Bo*" (administration over maritime trade) and "*Shi Bo Shi*" (Maritime Trade Supervisor) are two different concepts. From the perspective of literature, they both appeared in the Tang Dynasty[2]. At present, most of the research focuses on "*Shi Bo Shi*" and many papers have been published, but research on "*Shi Bo*" which is an administrative behavior over maritime trade is actually of more important value. It had been a tradition since the Southern Dynasties that the local chief executives of Guangzhou and their subordinates were in charge of the shipping. In the 2nd year of Kaiyuan period (714 AD), Emperor Xuanzong of the Tang Dynasty sent *Shi Bo Shi* to participate in the shipping business. During the reign of Emperor Dezong of the Tang Dynasty, *Shi Bo Shi* was assumed concurrently by *Jian Jun* (army overseers), which changed from the original temporary to the relatively fixed permanent emissary post. Wei Guangrun's *Jin Ling Nan Wang Guan Shi Bo Shi Yuan Tu Biao (Chart of the Shi Bo Shi Courtyard in Nanwang Embassy of Lingnan)* gave a brief description of the buildings in the courtyard, which recorded the historical facts that the old Haiyang embassy was renovated and transformed into

[2] Li Hu, Shi Bo Shi and Shi Bo Administration in the Tang Dynasty, *Historical Research*, 1998(3).

the courtyard of *Shi Bo Shi*. Since then, *Shi Bo Shi* had a fixed office[3]. However, the location recorded is at the Pearl River side far away from the excavation area of the palace site.

Besides the courtyard of *Shi Bo Shi*, another name of the state government office that can be searched in the literature is *Xiang Jun Tang* (the Hall to Entertain Military) of Lingnan region. In Liu Zongyuan's work, it was another building closely related to the Maritime Silk Road. It was an important place to entertain foreign guests which was located in *Du Fu* (the abbreviation of *Du Du Fu*), the agency of the highest authority in Lingnan road. In December of the 8th year of Yuanhe period (813 AD), Ma Zong, *Ci Shi* of Guangzhou and *Jie Du Shi* of Lingnan Road, rebuilt *Xiang Jun Tang* to hold a great feast so as to attract bussiness and build prestige. In the following year, Liu Zongyuan was invited to write *Ling Nan Jie Du Xiang Jun Tang Ji (Record of Xiang Jun Tang in Lingnan)* which recorded the enormous scale of the hall and the grand occasion of the feast. More than one thousand envoys and merchants from countries like Daxia and Kangju of Central Asia, Heling of the South China Sea, and Liuqiu of the East China Sea attended the ceremony.

The cultural layer of the Tang Dynasty excavated at the palace site of Nanyue state contained many relics and remains such as foundation sites, roads, wells and so on. The foundation sites were unable to correspond with the offices of *Du Du* and *Jie Du Shi* due to the lack of written materials.

Unearthed cultural relics of the Tang Dynasty related to the Maritime Silk Road are the important historical products - porcelain for export - rather than imported goods. The large capacity of seagoing vessels made ceramics a bulk export commodity. According to research results of predecessors and modern people, since the middle Tang Dynasty, Chinese ceramics have been found in large amount along the *"Guangzhou Tong Hai Yi Dao"* which was a routine from Guangzhou to Sri Lanka, India, the Persian Gulf, the Arabian Peninsula, and East Africa along the Indo-China Peninsula, the Indonesian Islands and via the Malacca Strait. Many similar objects were also unearthed in Guangzhou, fully showing that Guangzhou played a role as a departure port. In the Tang Dynasty, Guangzhou was the only city where *Shi Bo Shi* was dispatched. However, whether the transportation and trade of the South China Sea could only be carried out from Guangzhou cannot be judged yet due to the lack of empirical materials.

Study of maritime transportation and trade in academic circle mainly takes the Tang and Song Dynasties as a unit. This is because the Tang and Song Dynasties comprise a transformation period of China's political structure and political system (the innovation in Tang and Song Dynasties). It is particularly important that shipping administration was implemented, formally incorporating overseas transportation and trade into the legal administration system. However, as far as the administration system is concerned, there were many differences between Tang Dynasty and Song Dynasty. In early Tang Dynasty, the administration mode was local administrative officials taking

[3] Huang Lou, Research on the Author and Time of Jin Ling Nan Wang Guan Shi Bo Shi Yuan Tu Biao: Along with Related Problems Like the Responsibility and Evolution of Shi Bo Shi in the Tang Dynasty, *Journal of Sun Yat-Sen University (Social Science Edition)*, 2009(2). That paper argued that the author of the chart was Wei Guangrun rather than Wang Qianxiu as said before.

the charge, following that of the Southern Dynasties, while in the middle stage, *Shi Bo Shi* and *Jian Jun Shi* were sent to participate in shipping administration, thus creating a new administration mode. The latter method was inherited and developed by the Song Dynasty. In Song, regulations on shipping were first made and then inherited by the Yuan Dynasty.

The Song Dynasty was the first to set up a maritime trade administration in Guangzhou. In the 4th year of Kaibao period (971AD), when the Southern Han Dynasty was conquered, it was already ten years since the founding of the Song Dynasty. It can be said that *Shi Bo Si* was established just because Guangzhou was under control and the establishment was based on the already developed overseas trade of Guangzhou in the Tang and Five Dynasties. The shipping administration of Song improved from dispatching envoys to establishing special department, and in the 3rd year of Yuanfeng period (1080 AD), regulations on shipping in Guangzhou were revised.

The overseas trade of the Song Dynasty can be divided into two ways: government administration and merchant management, which greatly changed the trade type and structure. The Song and Yuan Dynasties witnessed the most prosperous period of non-governmental overseas trade. During the middle Yongxi period, Emperor Taizong of the Song Dynasty sent eight servants carrying gold, silk and imperial edicts to attract people of the South China Sea countries via four routes, encouraging merchants to go abroad and sell goods in foreign countries. Chinese and Western historical and travel records of Song and Yuan Dynasties were more abundant than those of the previous dynasties, while there were relatively fewer related relics unearthed. Since the late Tang Dynasty, a large number of spices were imported, and the transaction of luxury goods such as jewels was replaced by exporting commercial ceramics in bulk. With the further development in Song and Yuan Dynasties, there were fewer imported artifacts such as pearls, gold and silver found in archaeological excavations. At the same time, Buddhism had also been Sinicized while declining in India, and the number of overseas Buddhist relics also decreased. There were more than 410 kinds of import and export goods in the Song Dynasty, which can be divided into treasures, cloth, fragrant goods, leather goods, groceries, medicinal materials, and so on. As far as imported spices were concerned, there were more than 100 kinds of names and colors. However, these goods were precisely ones that can hardly found in archaeological excavations.

In the Song Dynasty cultural layer of the palace site of Nanyue state, a large number of porcelains produced in domestic kilns were discovered, which was undoubtedly a proof that vessels departed from Guangzhou at that time. Meanwhile, it can also be seen that the number of wares from northern kilns was relatively smaller than those of southern kilns, indicating that goods were exported at different ports in the Song Dynasty. As other scholars have pointed out, to meet the needs of overseas markets, porcelains for export were not merely exported, but were also for the use of local residents. Cultural relics found in the house foundation sites and water wells were enough to prove the situation. Porcelains in the shape with foreign cultural factors were exported and used by domestic people as well, which increased the interest of life and changed aesthetic concepts.

When talking about Guangzhou being an important port of China's Maritime Silk Road for more than two thousand years without interruption, the biggest query is that Quanzhou surpassed and replaced Guangzhou in overseas transportation and trade from the late Southern Song Dynasty to the early Yuan Dynasty.

In the 4th year of Kaibao period (971 AD), Emperor Taizu of the Song Dynasty set up the first *Shi Bo Si* in Guangzhou (Guangnan East Road *Shi Bo Si*), which operated until the 1st year of Xiangxing period (1278 AD) at the end of the Southern Song Dynasty, lasting for more than 300 years. In the 2nd year of Yuanyou period (1087 AD), Fujian Road *Shi Bo Si* was added in Quanzhou and lasted for nearly 200 years until 1276 AD when the Southern Song Dynasty collapsed. All the departments were set up after the establishment of Guangzhou *Shi Bo Si*, forming a pattern that Guangzhou was the leading one and followed by Quanzhou, Mingzhou and Hangzhou.

Before the establishment of *Shi Bo Si* in Quanzhou, merchants of Quanzhou needed to apply for a certificate in Liangzhe or Guangdong *Shi Bo Si* if wanting to go to the sea. "When merchants went to sea to sell goods in foreign countries, they had to ask Liangzhe *Shi Bo Si* for official certificates, and the goods of those who had no certificate would have to be confiscated." "People of Quanzhou who trade overseas had to inform to Guangdong *Shi Bo Si* when departed and returned, or the goods would be confiscated." In the 3rd year of Yuanfeng period (1080 AD), regulations on shipping in Guangzhou stipulated that those vessels going to the South China Sea which were not approved by Guangzhou *Shi Bo Si* and those going to Japan and Koryo which were not approved by Mingzhou *Shi Bo Si* were all illegal. It can be seen that though maritime transportation and trade of Quanzhou made great progress in the Song Dynasty, it was still behind Guangzhou and Ningbo[4].

In 1974, a wooden boat of Southern Song Dynasty was excavated at Houzhu port in Quanzhou, Fujian Province. A number of cultural relics including spices that were related to the Maritime Silk Road were found on the boat. Archaeologists and historians actively discussed Quanzhou's historical status as an ancient trading port in China based on the findings. Some scholars put forward that "at least in the late Southern Song Dynasty, Quanzhou was the main gateway for Jiangsu, Zhejiang and Fujian to trade overseas. Quanzhou port was in a trend of gradually surpassing Guangzhou and becoming the first overseas trade port", and "the war between Song and Jin and the migration of the Song court to the South were important political factors for the rise of Quanzhou port in the Southern Song Dynasty"[5]. Some studies also pointed out that during Shaoding period of Emperor Lizong (1228-1233 AD), the special department administrating shipping trade in Quanzhou was eventually cancelled due to the recession of trade, replaced by Quanzhou Prefect concurrently taking charge of the bussiness. At the end of the Southern Song Dynasty, Quanzhou *Shi Bo Si* was cancelled as the local shipping trade declined extremely. In fact, in the late Southern Song Dynasty, shipping trade in Quanzhou and Guangzhou both declined. However, Quanzhou declined rapidly,

[4] Reference about commercial ceramics lies in *Research on Shi Bo Si in the Song Dynasty* written by Yang Wenxin, Xiamen University Press, 2013.

[5] Wu Tai & Chen Gaohua, Overseas Trade in Song and Yuan Dynasties along with the Prosperity and Decline of Quanzhou Port, *Journal of Maritime History Studies*, 1978(1).

while Guangzhou did much slower[6].

In terms of historical materials, Quanzhou was undoubtedly an important foreign trade port in the Southern Song and Yuan Dynasties. In Southern Song, Quanzhou was closer to the capital Lin'an than Guangzhou, so its status rose. In Yuan, due to the policy of protecting the interests of officials, shipping magnates gathered in the south of the Yangtze River to take the advantage of the Grand Canal and offshore, which made Quanzhou obtain a strong momentum of development. Different from Quanzhou *Shi Bo Si*, vessels of Guangzhou only went to the South China Sea, while those of Quanzhou could went to the South China Sea via Guangzhou or to the East Ocean via Mingzhou.

In Vol.7 of *Da De Nan Hai Zhi, Bo Huo (Cargo on Board)*, written by Chen Dazhen of the Yuan Dynasty, it was recorded that Guangzhou was a place where many foreign vessels as well as treasures and cargos gathered. It was like a foreign city. Strange people and animals, together with treasures like dragon beads, rhinoceros and shells, were all stored in the government office and kept in the gardens. According to the book, the number of countries that could be reached from Guangzhou via the sea was 147, far more than the previous dynasties. Just like Quanzhou, Qingyuan and other ports transporting all kinds of overseas goods to the capital, there were also a large number of treasures transported to the imperial court from Guangzhou. Although the pattern of maritime transportation and trade changed greatly in Song and Yuan Dynasties with more overseas ports and more trade forms like officials and civil people going abroad separately, it did not affect Guangzhou's position as the largest port to the South China Sea.

At the beginning of the Ming Dynasty, *Shi Bo Ti Ju Si* were respectively set up in Ningbo, Quanzhou and Guangzhou. Ningbo was designated to connect Japan, Quanzhou to Ryukyu, and Guangzhou to Champa, Siam and the western countries. From the perspective of the regional scope in charge by these *Shi Bo Si*, Guangzhou administrated a vast area from the Southeast Asia to the West. In the Ming Dynasty, cancellation of other *Shi Bo Si* happened frequently, while Guangzhou *Shi Bo Si* was kept open. Zhu Yuanzhang changed the policy of free overseas trade of the former dynasties, implemented the policy of closing the customs and banning going to the sea, and established the coastal defense system to prepare for the war. He issued a decree that people near the sea were not allowed to go to sea without permission, which greatly hit the strength of China's maritime merchants. After Zheng He's voyages to the West, China's official vessels no longer appeared in the Indian Ocean. However, folk overseas trade was unstoppable, and still maintained the dominant position in the Southeast Asian market.

After quelling the San Fan revolt and unifying Taiwan, Emperor Kangxi of the Qing Dynasty lifted the three-hundred-year ban on maritime trade since the Ming Dynasty, and carried out the policy of opening up maritime trade. In the 24th year of Kangxi period (1685 AD), four big customs were officially established which were Guangzhou Yue customs, Xiamen Min customs, Ningbo Zhe customs and Shanghai Jiang customs. In the 22nd year of Qianlong period (1757 AD), the British

[6] Zhang Shen, Preliminary Investigation of Shi Bo Si in the Southern Song Dynasty, *Academic Research*, 1992(5).

merchant fleet arrived at Ningbo port of Zhejiang Province. Although there existed customs in Ningbo, it was not for foreign vessels to dock, let alone that Ningbo was an important coastal defense area, so the Qing court believed that foreign vessels should not be allowed to enter and leave Fujian and Zhejiang areas. Qianlong issued a decree that the port for foreign vessels was set in Guangdong, and no more foreign vessels were allowed to go to Zhejiang Province. Min, Zhe and Jiang customs stopped trade between China and the West, resulting in European and American vessels all gathering at Yue customs. "Four ports for trade" thus became "one port for trade". This policy continued until the Opium War. Under the threat of the gunboats of the great powers, "five ports for trade" policy was carried out in Guangzhou, Xiamen, Fuzhou, Ningbo and Shanghai.

The monopoly of import and export trade for nearly one hundred years generated the most prosperous period of foreign trade at Guangzhou port. After the establishment of Yue customs, Thirteen-hong of Canton was officially established. More than ten commercial firms of Guangzhou franchised for foreign trade since the Qing court lifted the ban on maritime trade were included. In the 23rd year of Daoguang period (1843 AD), Thirteen-hong of Canton was destroyed in a fire. Today, people can only recall the brilliance of that time through the names of several firms left on Thirteen-hong Road.

III

The purpose of holding this exhibition is to expound the relationship between archaeological remains and the Maritime Silk Road. The palace site of Nanyue state is the royal palace of Nanyue state from the 3rd to the 2nd century BC and Nanan state in the 10th century, as well as the government office of the other dynasties. Policies were also issued here, which cannot be directly observed from the archaeological site and the cultural relics unearthed due to the lack of written records. The exhibition should not only be a display of relics, but also a combination with documents, historical events and historical figures, so as to tell the formation and development of the Maritime Silk Road. Its content should not be limited to the archaeological site itself, but need to be expanded to more aspects to show the complete features of the history of maritime communication. Therefore, it is necessary to absorb the latest research results and add cultural relics that are not unearthed in but closely related to Guangzhou. For example, the three silver bars unearthed in 1989 in western suburb of Xi'an of Shaanxi Province were the legacy of Ishaq, a Persian merchant, which were paid to Emperor Dezong of the Tang Dynasty as tributes by Guangzhou officials. Among them, one bar inscribed the name Zhang Boyi who was *Ci Shi* of Guangzhou and deputy *Jie Du Shi* of Lingnan, and the name Liu Chujiang who was *Jian Jun* and *Shi Bo Shi* of Lingnan, showing that the overseas trade of the Tang Dynasty was jointly supervised by *Jie Du Shi* and *Shi Bo Shi*, with *Jie Du Shi* as the chief and *Shi Bo Shi* as the assistant[7]. Another example is the gravestone of Yang Liangyao, which was

[7] Li Jinxiu, Research on Overseas Trade Administration in the Tang Dynasty from the Silver Bars of Persian Ishaq, *Historical Science of Jinan University*, No.8, Guangxi Normal University Press, 2013.

found in Jingyang County, Shaanxi Province in 1984. Yang Liangyao was sent as an envoy to Hei Yi Da Shi (Abbasid Caliphate) from the South China Sea in the 1st year of Zhengyuan period (785 AD) during of the reign of Emperor Dezong of the Tang Dynasty. This is the earliest exact record of the Tang Dynasty sending envoys to sail to the West[8].

Another breakthrough of this exhibition is the introduction of people who made outstanding contributions to overseas trade administration. Relevant figures of the past dynasties are selected according to historical records and portraits are created based on major events, so as to more vividly and concretely tell the audience about the deeds of the historical figures and their contributions to the development of the Maritime Silk Road.

The South China Sea has been the sea way of China's foreign transportation and trade ever since the Qin and Han Dynasties. There were rich historical materials of the Maritime Silk Road in Buddhist documents, and there were many records of Indian Buddhists coming to China to preach through Guangzhou. Fa Xian in the Eastern Jin Dynasty was the first person to reach India from China, and also the first person to return to China via the sea. At the beginning of Tang Dynasty, Yi Jing was also an eminent monk who went to India to fetch scriptures from Guangzhou. Fa Xian and Yi Jing were both symbolic figures of the early Maritime Silk Road.

The implementation of the shipping trade administration policies lies in people, and the historical figures represented by government officials are selected due to their roles played in maritime transportation and trade administration, including positive and negative aspects. According to historical records, the selection criterion of the figures is whether their contributions to the maritime trade administration during their work in Guangzhou can be handed down by legends or relics. For example, Wu Yinzhi in the Western Jin Dynasty is a government official who had a direct relationship with the Maritime Silk Road as recorded in historical documents. His poem about *Tan Quan* (the Spring of Greed) and historical remains reflect his determination to remedy the abuse of the former officials often embezzling goods, which had a profound impact on later generations. In Tang Dynasty, many poems mentioned *Tan Quan* were often related to overseas treasures.

As early as in the Song Dynasty, there were already shrines established for incorruptible officials related to overseas trade. The preface of *Nan Hai Bai Yong · Shi Xian Ci (One Hundred Poems of the South China Sea · Shrine of the Ten Sages)* said that Wu Yinzhi, Song Jing, Li Shangyin, Lu Huan, Li Mian, Kong Qian, Lu Diao and Xiao Fang were often regarded as the eight sages of the former prefect, while Jiang Yingshu added Teng Xiu and Wang Chen to build the shrine of the ten sages. Jiang wrote preface himself and engraved the names and preface onto the stone. There was also another shrine of the eight sages, including Ge Panmei, Xiang Minzhong, Yu Jing, Wei Guan, Shao Yu, Chen Shiqing, Chen Congyi and Zhang Jie, which was built by the commander-in-chief Zhou Ziqiang.

---

[8] Zhang Shimin, Yang Liangyao: The First Chinese Envoy to Sail to the West, *Journal of Xianyang Normal University*, Vol. 20, 2005(3).

Lu Sigong, who was appointed as Lingnan *Jie Du Shi* in the 8th year of Dali period of the Tang Dynasty (773 AD), was a negative figure. Lu made contributions in quelling the rebellion of Geshu Huang, yet he killed overseas merchants and took possession of the millions of wealth confiscated, which aroused the resentment of Emperor Dezong of the Tang Dynasty. In the house of Yuan Zai, the then prime minister, a foreign glass dish with a diameter of up to 10 *Cun* bribed by Lu Sigong was confiscated, the size of which is comparable to the glass dish unearthed in the underground palace of Famen temple.

It should be noted that in the Ming and Qing Dynasties, a large number of foreign trade commodities, such as Chinese silk, porcelain and tea, were exported by foreign vessels, and Western instruments, handicrafts and works of art were also introduced to China, forming a new pattern of communication between the East and the West. Since this exhibition is based on archaeological materials, and there are rich collections in other museums of Guangdong Province and many such special exhibitions have been held, so this part of content is relatively less involved.

IV

A number of relics, remains and ancient buildings with foreign cultural factors, including religious cultural remains like Buddhist temples, churches and cemeteries, are all material evidence of the Maritime Silk Road and key points in understanding and the study of the Maritime Silk Road. However, no settlements and places for activities of foreign merchants, together with ancient trade ports and wharves that could most directly reflect the Maritime Silk Road have been officially excavated yet, and the location as well as shape and structure of such remains have not been confirmed either, which is undoubtedly a great pity.

There are still many academic problems to be solved, and the research is not deep enough. For example, there are many archaeological materials indicating the folk communication in the Qin and Han Dynasties, while the official diplomatic behaviors of the Qin Dynasty and Nanyue state still need more materials to demonstrate. Another example is the situation of the Persian ship "Blackstone" when it came to China for trade, which was discovered in Indonesian waters. There are opinions of Guangzhou and Yangzhou as the port cities of its docking and departure. From the perspective of the shipping development situation in the Tang Dynasty, we tend to accept the opinion of Guangzhou, yet we still lack comprehensive research on port cities in the Tang Dynasty, especially on the administration mode of foreign vessels in the Tang Dynasty. Were the foreign trade ports limited at that time, and if so, to which cities?

The three volumes *The Maritime Silk Road · Guangzhou Cultural Heritage* compiled in 2007 are just data compilation. Mr. Mai Yinghao repeatedly stressed the importance of making good use of these materials to compile the history of the Maritime Silk Road. This requires more efforts and manpower from the relics and museology system of Guangzhou, and young people need to be encouraged to join the research team of cultural relics. All the units concerned should also work together with academic research institutions as well as domestic and foreign universities to push the research on the Maritime Silk Road to a new level.

Finally, I would like to put forward my views on the naming of the Maritime Silk Road historical sites in Guangzhou which are applying for the world cultural heritage. At present, the application text takes "the palace site of Nanyue and Nanhan states" as the name of the site and project. This name highlights the direct administration of maritime trade by local regimes in the 3rd to 2nd Centuries B.C. and the 10th century AD, but weakens the administration pattern of the central government - local officials and envoys in other historical periods, thus failing to fully manifest the history of Guangzhou as the largest port city of the East on the South China Sea Maritime Silk Road. Guangzhou's maritime foreign transportation and trade have lasted for two thousand years since the Qin and Han Dynasties, which is very unique in China.

The palace site of Nanyue state is an archaeological name based on the nature of the site during excavation in the 20th century. However, it comprises stratigraphic accumulation and historical remains of 12 dynasties, which was the political and cultural center and maritime trade administration agency of Lingnan area in different historical periods, and witnessed the prosperity of Guangzhou port relying on the Maritime Silk Road. The "uninterrupted" that was said above is referred to the continuity of the administrative power. At present, the palace site of Nanyue state is the only one that can reflect all the development stages. Through the unearthed objects and historical documents, we can know about and understand the development and evolution of the Maritime Silk Road in China. However, the preservation situation of ancient cultural relics is not optimistic. As Guangzhou is the central city of Lingnan area with rapid economic development, many of the previous and contemporary historical remains and relics vanished due to the acceleration of urban renewal. Together with the two-thousand -year natural and man-made destruction, many important historical relics have been annihilated, with only a small part of the cultural remains and relics of the Maritime Silk Road extant. Considering these factors, the preservation, utilization and display of the relics of the palace site of Nanyue state become even more precious. Therefore, it fully conforms to the authenticity standard to use the archaeological cultural name and take the conventionally established "the palace site of Nanyue state" as the name to apply for the world cultural heritage. What's more, it can more comprehensively show its durability and relevance with the Maritime Silk Road, which conforms more to the 3rd standard of applying for the world cultural heritage, that is, to provide a unique or at least special witness for a vanished civilization or cultural tradition.

Curator of Archaeological Site Museum of Nanyue Palace: Quan Hong

前 言

　　"海上丝绸之路"是古代人们借助季风与洋流等自然条件，利用风帆航海技术开展贸易的海上大通道，也是东西方文化交流、传播与融合的对话之路。

　　广州古称番禺，是秦汉时期的九大都会之一，是海外珠玑、象牙、犀角、玳瑁的重要集散地，是中国海上丝绸之路最早形成的港口城市之一。

　　自 20 世纪 90 年代以来，在广州市中山四路考古发现了西汉南越国、五代十国南汉国的都城、王宫以及历代官署遗迹，出土了一批具有东南亚、南亚和西亚等海外文化因素的遗物。南越国—南汉国宫署遗址是广州两千多年来岭南地区政治、经济、文化中心和海上贸易管理机构所在地，是中国海上丝绸之路兴起、发展和繁荣历史变迁的重要历史见证。

　　广州位于亚洲大陆的东南端，面向南海，地当西、北、东三江出海交汇处，是珠江三角洲经济核心区，具有便捷的内河交通以及适宜发展海上交通的亚热带季风气候等优异的自然条件。凭借地缘优势，广州在秦汉时期快速崛起，成为沟通中国内陆并联通海外的重要海陆交通枢纽城市。

　　南越国—南汉国宫署遗址位于广州历史城区中心，文化层堆积厚达 5～6 米，包含秦、汉（含南越国）、三国、两晋、南朝、隋、唐、五代十国南汉国、宋、元、明、清、民国等 13 个历史时期的文化遗存，见证了广州自海上丝绸之路形成之日起，历经两千多年海外商贸与文化交流持续发展和繁荣的历程。

Preface

　　The Maritime Silk Road was an important maritime route where the ancient people utilized natural conditions (such as monsoons and ocean currents) and sail navigation technologies to conduct trade activities. It was also a route of dialogue that facilitated cultural exchange, communication and integration between the Eastern and Western countries.

　　Guangzhou was known as Panyu in ancient times. It was one of the nine metropolises in the Qin and Han Dynasties and for a long time, served as a collecting and distributing center of overseas pearls, ivory, rhino horns and tortoiseshell. It was one of the earliest port cities along the Maritime Silk Road.

　　Since the 1990s, remains of the capitals and palaces of Nanyue state of the Western Han Dynasty and Nanhan state of the Five Dynasties and Ten Kingdoms Period, as well as government offices of multiple dynasties, have been discovered in the archaeological excavations along Zhongshan 4th Road, with a number of relics embodying cultural elements of Southeast Asia, South Asia and West Asia unearthed. The palace site of Nanyue and Nanhan states is an important historical witness not only of Guangzhou being the center of politics, economy and culture and the location of the administrative agency for maritime trade in Lingnan region for more than 2,000 years, but also of the rise, development and prosperity of the Maritime Silk Road.

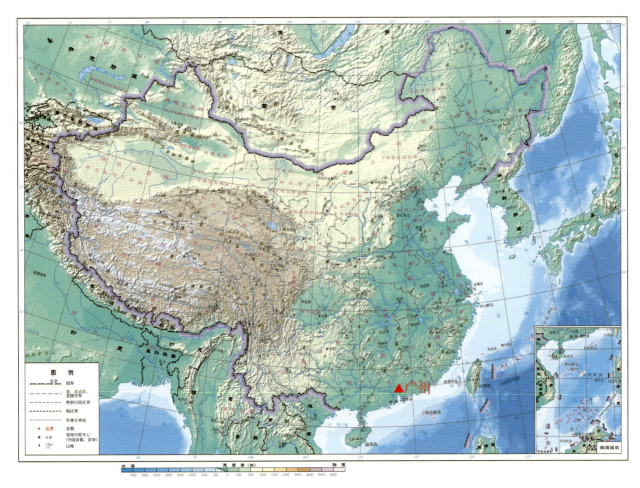

广州在中国的位置
Guangzhou's Position in China

Located in the southeast tip of the Asian continent and facing the South China Sea, Guangzhou lies in the place where Xijiang, Beijiang and Dongjiang rivers intersect. As the center of the Pearl River Delta economic zone, it is blessed with convenient inland waterway transportation, as well as subtropical monsoon climate and other excellent natural conditions that are suitable for the development of maritime transportation. Given its geographic advantages, Guangzhou emerged rapidly in Qin and Han Dynasties into an important sea and land transportation hub connecting inland China and the rest of the world.

The palace site of Nanyue and Nanhan states is located in the center of the historic urban area of Guangzhou, with cultural layers 5-6 meters thick, covering 13 historical periods including Qin, Han (including Nanyue state), the Three Kingdoms, Eastern and Western Jin, the Southern Dynasties, Sui, Tang, the Five Dynasties and Ten Kingdoms (Nanhan state), Song, Yuan, Ming, Qing and the Republic of China. It is the witness of the history of the development and flourishing of maritime trade and cultural exchange of Guangzhou for more than 2,000 years the birth of since the Maritime Silk Road.

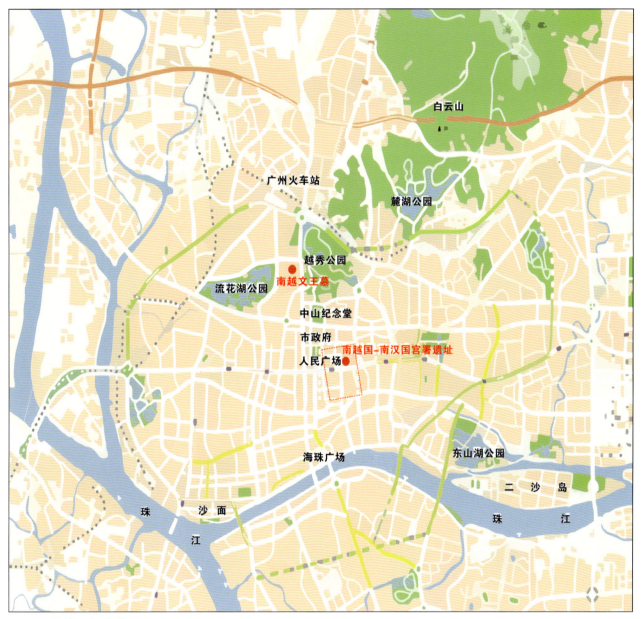

─────南越国都城范围

南越国—南汉国宫署遗址位置示意图
Map of the Palace Site of Nanyue and Nanhan States

广州 · 海上丝绸之路大事年表

前 214 年	秦统一岭南，设南海郡，郡治番禺（今广州）。
前 203 年	赵佗建立南越国，以番禺为都城。
226 年	孙权"分交州置广州"，广州由此得名。
226~231 年	孙权遣使经广州出使林邑、扶南（今越南中南部）等国。
607 年	隋炀帝派常骏等由广州出使赤土（今马来半岛）。
671 年	唐高僧义净从广州沿海上丝绸之路到印度取经。
714 年	唐朝在广州设市舶使管理海外贸易。
917 年	刘岩以广州为都城建立南汉国，积极发展海外贸易。
971 年	北宋首在广州设市舶司管理海外贸易。
1523 年	明朝废罢泉州、宁波市舶司，保留广东市舶司，刺激民间私人贸易。
1757~1842 年	清政府实施广州"一口通商"政策，规定西洋、南洋番船、番商只在广东通商。

Guangzhou · Chronicle of the Maritime Silk Road

214 BC	Lingnan region was brought under the control of the Qin Empire and Nanhai Prefecture was established, with Panyu (present Guangzhou) as the capital.
203 BC	Zhao Tuo established Nanyue state, with Panyu as the capital.
226 AD	Guangzhou (Guang Province) was separated from Jiaozhou (Jiao Province) by Sun Quan and Guangzhou has got its current name since then.
226-231 AD	Sun Quan sent ambassadors to Linyi (LâmÂp in Vietnamese, a kingdom in present central Vietnam) and Funan (central and south Vietnam) via Guangzhou.
607 AD	Emperor Yang of the Sui Dynasty sent Chang Jun as an ambassador to Chitu (a kingdom in Malay Peninsula) via Guangzhou.
671 AD	In Tang Dynasty, Monk Yijing started his pilgrim journey to India from Guangzhou.
714 AD	In Tang Dynasty, the post of *Shi Bo Shi* (Maritime Trade Supervisor) was established to supervise overseas trade.
917 AD	Nanhan state was established by Liu Yan with Guangzhou as its capital. The new state attached great importance to the development of overseas trade.
971 AD	In Northern Song Dynasty, the first *Shi Bo Si* (Maritime Trade Bureau) was established in Guangzhou to supervise overseas trade.
1523 AD	In Ming Dynasty, Quanzhou and Ningbo *Shi Bo Si* (Maritime Trade Bureaus) were closed while Guangdong *Shi Bo Si* remained, leaving a great opportunity for the development of non-governmental trade.
1757-1842 AD	The policy of single-port-commerce system was imposed to restrict trade with foreign ships and merchants from the west and from the south Pacific conducted only in Guangdong.

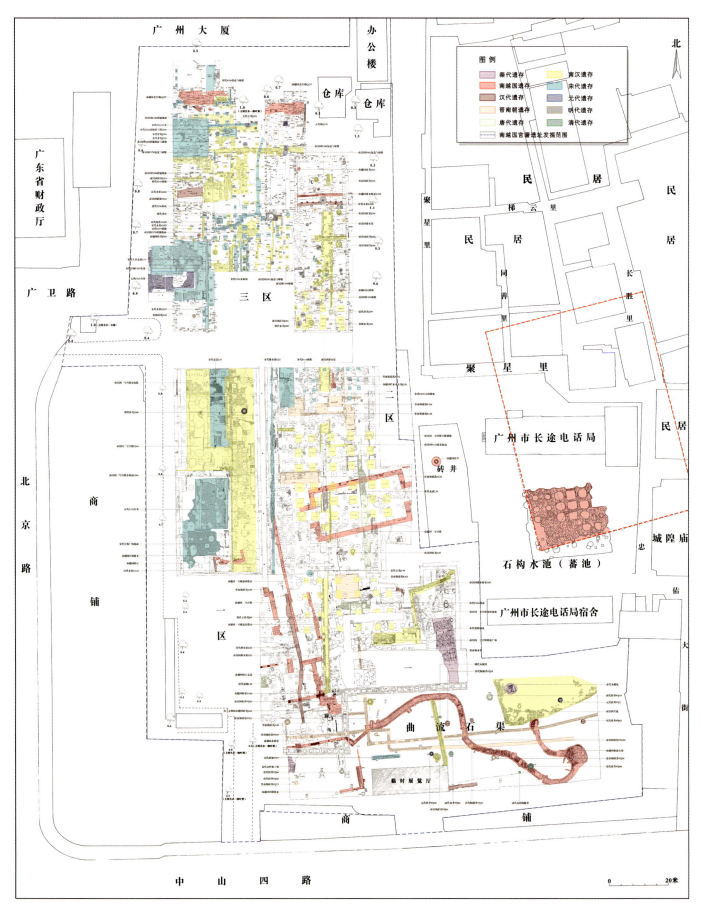

南越国—南汉国宫署遗址历代重要遗迹平面图
Plan of Significant Historical Remains of Different Dynasties in the Palace Site of Nanyue and Nanhan States

南越国—南汉国宫署遗址文化层

Cultural Layers of the Palace Site of Nanyue and Nanhan States

　　秦始皇三十三年（公元前214年）统一岭南，置桂林、南海、象三郡，南海郡治番禺（今广州），为广州信史记载的建城之始。

　　西汉早期，在岭南地区建立的南越国，经过近百年的积极经营与大力开发，社会、经济和文化取得了巨大发展。南越国还通过开通海上交通与其他地区进行海上贸易和文化交流，使都城番禺快速崛起成为海外珍宝的重要集散地和繁华的大都会，开启了中国海上丝绸之路历史先河。

In the 33rd year of the reign of Qin Shi Huang (214 BC), the First Emperor of Qin, Lingnan region was brought entirely under the control of the empire. The Qin court established Guilin, Nanhai and Xiang Commanderies. Panyu (present Guangzhou) is made the capital of Nanhai Commandery and it is the beginning of Guangzhou as a city in recorded history.

In the early Western Han Dynasty, Nanyue Kingdom, established in Lingnan Region, had made great progress in social, economic and cultural development after nearly a century of diligent cultivation. Taking advantage of the newly established sailing routes, followed by maritime trade and cultural exchange with other parts of the world, the capital Panyu was quickly developed into a distribution center for overseas rare goods and a bustling metropolis, marking the beginning of the tradition of China's Maritime Silk Road.

岭南都会
A Metropolis in Lingnan Region

秦始皇兼并六国后，于公元前 219 年派兵进攻南越，公元前 214 年平定南越，建立起中国历史上第一个统一的多民族国家。

秦末，中原战乱，原秦南海郡尉赵佗为了维护岭南社会稳定，发兵击并桂林、象郡，于公元前 203 年建立南越国，定都番禺。《汉书》记载，番禺是秦汉时期九大都会之一。

自 1995 年以来，在南越国宫署遗址先后考古发掘出南越国的宫苑和宫殿遗迹，确证遗址所在地是两千年前南越国政权的中枢所在。

After the conquest of six states, Qin Shi Huang, the First Emperor of Qin sent his army to conquer the Yue tribes in 219 BC and in 214 BC, the Yue tribes were annexed to the empire. For the first time in Chinese history, a unified and multi-ethnic country was established.

In late Qin dynasty, revolts broke out in the Central Plains Region (an area on the lower reaches of the Yellow River which is the center of Chinese civilization and politics) and Zhao Tuo, the former General of Nanhai Commandery, attacked Guilin and Xiang Commanderies and made them subjugated in order to maintain stability of Lingnan Region. In 203 BC, he found the independent kingdom of Nanyue and made Panyu its capital. According to the *Book of Han*, Panyu was one of the nine metropolises during Qin and Han dynasties.

Since 1995, royal garden and palaces of Nanyue Kingdom were unearthed in archaeological excavations at the site of Nanyue Kingdom Palace Site, confirming that it was exactly the location of the central government of Nanyue Kingdom which can be dated back to 2,000 years ago.

汉《淮南子·人间训》中有关秦始皇发兵进攻岭南的记载
In the chapter of *Ren Jian Xun* of *Huai Nan Zi*, which was complied in the Han Dynasty, the military conquest of Emperor Shi Huang of the Qin Dynasty in Lingnan region was recorded as follows.

《汉书》中关于番禺的记载
The Record of panyu in the chapter of *Han shu* (*the History of the Han Dynasty*)

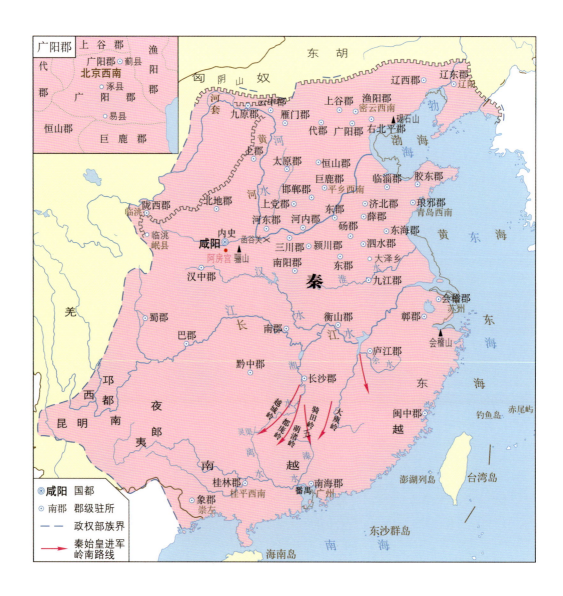

秦始皇进军岭南路线示意图
Map of Routes Showing How the Army of Emperor Shi Huang of
the Qin Dynasty Attacked Lingnan Region

铜戈

战国（公元前 475 ~ 前 221 年）

通长 26、援长 16.3 厘米

铜戈内端一面刻有"十四年属邦工□戴丞□□□"十二字。十四年为秦始皇十四年，即公元前 233 年。铭文表明这把铜戈是由秦中央督造并为入越秦军配备的武器，是秦统一岭南的重要历史物证。

1962 年广州区庄螺岗西汉墓出土。

Bronze *Ge* (Dagger-axe)

The Warring States Period (475 BC-221 BC)

Total length: 26 cm / Length of yuan: 16.3 cm

One side of the dagger-axe was inscribed with 12 characters: *Shi Si Nian Shu Bang Gong* □ *Ji Cheng* □□□ . Shi Si Nian means the 14th year of Emperor Shi Huang's Reign, that is 233 BC. The inscription indicates that the bronze dagger-axe was manufactured under the supervision of the central government of Qin, and it was the weapon used by Qin soldiers who conquered the Nanyue tribes. It is an important evidence of the unification of Lingnan region in the Qin Dynasty.

It was unearthed from a tomb of the Western Han Dynasty in Quzhuang Luogang of Guangzhou in 1962.

陶壶

秦代（公元前 221 ~ 前 206 年）
口径 13.4、高 23.4 厘米

泥质灰陶，底部有烟灰痕。此陶壶为入越秦军携带的水器。
1996 年南越国宫署遗址出土。

Pottery Pot

The Qin Dynasty (221 BC-206 BC)
Mouth Diameter: 13.4 cm / Height: 23.4 cm

Grey pottery with soot mark remained at the bottom. This pot was a water vessel brought in
by the Qin army when conquering the Nanyue tribes.
It was unearthed at the Palace Site of Nanyue state in 1996.

陶釜

秦代（公元前 221 ~ 前 206 年）
口径 13.2、高 17.8 厘米

泥质灰陶，底部有烟灰痕。该陶釜是入越秦军携带的炊器。
1997 年南越国宫苑遗址出土。

Pottery Pot

The Qin Dynasty (221 BC-206 BC)
Mouth Diameter: 13.2 cm / Height: 17.8 cm

Grey pottery with soot mark remained at the bottom. This pot was a cooking vessel brought in by the Qin army when conquering the Nanyue tribes.
It was unearthed at the site of the royal garden of Nanyue state in 1997.

西汉时期南越国示意图
Map of the Nanyue State in the Western Han Dynasty
（说明：南越国属于西汉时期诸侯国，因地图出版审核的
需要，故在西汉时期疆域图上标示南越国的大致范围）

自公元前 203 年赵佗据有岭南建立南越国至公元前 111 年汉武帝灭南越，南越国共传四世五主，历 93 年，其疆域主要包括今广东、广西以及越南北部等地。

From Zhao Tuo's foundation of Nanyue state in Lingnan region in 203 BC to Emperor Wu of the Han Dynasty wiping out Nanyue state in 111 BC, the state had been passed on among five kings of four generations and existed for 93 years. Its territory extended from present Guangdong, Guangxi to northern Vietnam.

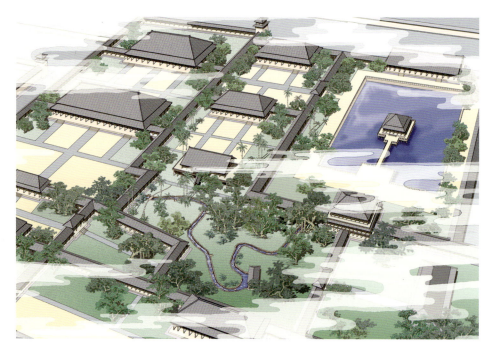

南越王宫遗址想象复原图
Imaginary Restoration Effect of the Palace of Nanyue State

　　自 1995 年以来，在广州市区先后发掘出南越国的宫苑、宫殿和宫墙遗迹，出土"华音宫"印文陶器盖、"殿中"封泥和南越木简等重要文物，证实遗址所在地为南越国的都城王宫核心区。

　　Since 1995, remains of royal garden, palaces and walls of Nanyue state have been unearthed in downtown Guangzhou, and the pottery lid printed with characters of "*Hua Yin Gong*" (Hua yin Palace), the clay seal with inscriptions of "*Dian Zhong*", along with wooden slips and many other relics have been excavated as evidence confirming that the site was the core area of the capital palaces of Nanyue state.

南越王宫遗址重要遗迹平面图
Plan of Important Remains in the Palace Site of Nanyue State

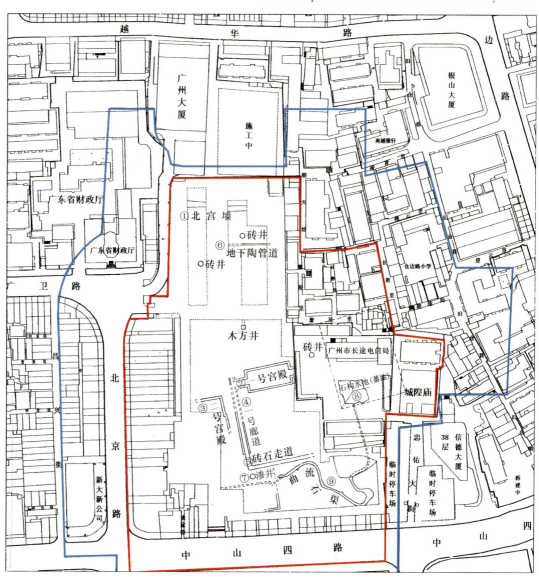

南越国一号宫殿为台基式建筑，平面呈长方形，东西长 30.2、南北宽 14.4 米，面积约 435 平方米。东、西两侧有入殿通道。台基四周散水宽 1.5 米，内侧铺大型印花砖，外侧铺砌碎石。殿内为经火烤的硬地面，根据残存的柱础石推测此建筑面阔七间、进深三间。

No.1 Palace of Nanyue state is built on a raised platform with a rectangular plane shape, which extends 30.2 meters from east to west and 14.4 meters from south to north. The total floor area is about 435 square meters. Corridors leading to the palace are available from both sides of the east and west. The water apron around the raised platform is 1.5 meters in width, paved with large stamped bricks on the inner side and gravels on the outskirt. The floor of the palace is hard clay roasted by fire. Judged by the remnants of the stone pedestals, the building should have seven trumeaux in length and three in depth.

南越国一号宫殿想象复原图
Imaginary Restoration Effect of No. 1 Palace of Nanyue State

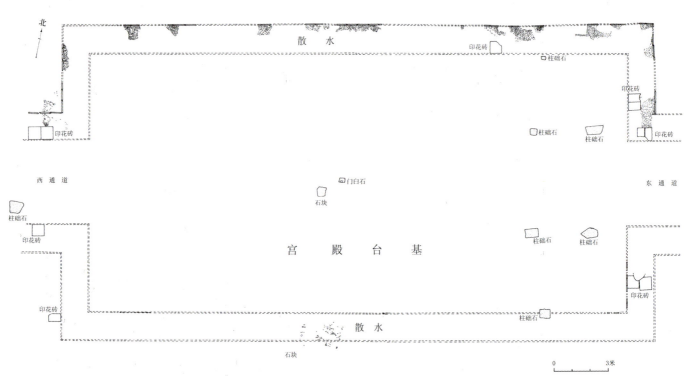

南越国一号宫殿基址平面图
Plan of the Site Base of No. 1 Palace of Nanyue State

殿内地面
Floor of the Palace

殿内柱础石
Stone Pedestal in the Palace

宫殿散水
Water Apron of the Palace

"横山" 木简

南越国时期（公元前 203 ~ 前 111 年）
残长 4.1、宽 1.8 厘米

2004 年，在南越国宫苑遗址西北部一口渗水井内清理出 100 多枚南越木简，内容涉及南越国纪年、地名、职官、宫室管理等。其中一枚简上墨书有"横山"两字，为南越国境内地名。经考证，位于岭南的横山有三处，分别在广东廉江县、广西忻城县和越南河静省。廉江横山位于北部湾安埔港，隔海与合浦相望，地位重要。越南横山位于今河静省东南海边，约当汉日南郡东北海隅。汉武帝元鼎六年（公元前 111 年）平南越，置十郡，其中的日南郡"辖境约当今越南中部北起横山、南抵大岭地区"。从所处地理位置看，木简上的"横山"应是汉日南郡的一处海上通商港口。

Heng Shan Wooden Slip

The Period of Nanyue state (203 BC-111 BC)
Residual length: 4.1 cm / width: 1.8 cm

In 2004, over 100 wooden slips of Nanyue state were discovered in a water-seeping well in the northwest part of the royal garden of Nanyue state. The inscriptions on the wooden slips contain records on calendar, names of places, appointment of officials, palace management, etc. One of the wooden slips has ink inscription of two characters on it: *Heng Shan*, which is the name of a place in the territory of Nanyue state. According to textual researches, there are three places named Hengshan in Lingnan region which are respectively in Lianjiang County of Guangdong Province, Xincheng County of Guangxi Province and Hà Tĩnh Province of Vietnam. Hengshan of Lianjiang County is located in Anpu Port of Beibu Gulf, the location of which is strategically important watching Hepu across the sea. Hengshan of Vietnam is located on the southeast coast of present Hà Tĩnh Province, which was the northeast corner of Rinan Prefecture of the Han Dynasty. In the 6th year of Yuanding Period of Emperor Wu of the Han Dynasty(111BC), ten prefectures were established after Nanyue state was wiped out, among which the jurisdiction area of Rinan Prefecture was from Hengshan to Daling area in present central Vietnam. Judged by the location, the inscribed *Heng Shan* should be a seaport in Rinan Prefecture.

木简

南越国时期（公元前 203 ~ 前 111 年）
长 22.6、宽 1.8 厘米

简文 "□张成故公主诞舍人廿六年七月属将常使□□□蕃禺人"。舍人即家臣，廿六年是南越王赵佗的纪年，即西汉文帝前元二年（公元前 178 年）。该木简是赵佗建立南越国的重要物证。

Wooden Slip

The Period of Nanyue state (203 BC-111 BC)
Length: 22.6 cm / Width: 1.8 cm

The text on the wooden slip reads: □ *Zhang Cheng Gu Gong Zhu Dan She Ren Nian Liu Nian Qi Yue Shu Jiang Chang Shi* □ □ □ *Pan Yu Ren* (Zhang Cheng, Princess Dan's former attendant, was appointed as an imperial bodyguard in July, the 26th year.) She Ren means attendant and Nian Liu Nian means the 26th year of the reign of Nanyue ruler Zhao Tuo, that is, the 2nd year of Qianyuan period of Emperor Wen of the Han Dynasty (178BC). This wooden slip is an important material evidence of Zhao Tuo's foundation of Nanyue state.

"华音宫"印文陶器盖

南越国时期（公元前 203 ~ 前 111 年）

印面长 2.8 厘米

赵佗建立南越国后仿效汉朝建有长乐、未央等宫殿，但"华音宫"
未见史籍记载，应是南越国自主设置的宫殿。

2003 年南越国宫署遗址出土。

Pottery Lid Printed with Characters of "*Hua Yin Gong*"

The Period of Nanyue state (203 BC-111 BC)

Seal Print Length: 2.8cm

After founding Nanyue state, Zhao Tuo named his palaces after palaces of the
Han Court, including Changle Palace and Weiyang Palace, but Huayin Palace
has never shown up in historical records. It is speculated to be a palace set up
according to Nanyue state's own need.

It was unearthed at the Palace Site of Nanyue state in 2003.

陶罐

南越国时期（公元前 203 ～前 111 年）

口径 20.3、高 26.6 厘米

印纹硬陶，为越人生产的本地陶器。

1997 年南越国宫苑遗址出土。

Pottery Jar

The Period of Nanyue state (203 BC-111 BC)

Mouth Diameter: 20.3 cm / Height: 26.6 cm

Stamped hard pottery made by local Yue people.

It was unearthed at the site of the royal garden of Nanyue state in 1997.

印花长方砖

南越国时期（公元前 203 ~ 前 111 年）
长 70、宽 45、厚 9 厘米

宫殿台基四周的散水铺砖。南越国宫殿用砖形式多样，大多模印精美的几何图案，
是"秦砖汉瓦"的杰出代表。
2009 年南越国宫署遗址出土。

Rectangular Brick with Stamped Pattern

The Period of Nanyue state (203 BC-111 BC)
Length: 70 cm/ Width: 45 cm/ Thickness: 9 cm

It is the paving brick of the water apron around the raised platform of the palace. Bricks of various
types were used in the palaces of Nanyue state and most of them were stamped with exquisite
geometric patterns. It is an outstanding example of "The Bricks and Tiles of the Qin and Han
Dynasties".
It was unearthed at the Palace Site of Nanyue state in 2009.

板瓦

南越国时期（公元前 203 ~ 前 111 年）

残长 46、最宽 37 厘米

板瓦宽大厚重，可见南越国宫殿建筑十分恢宏巍峨。
2002 年南越国宫署遗址出土。

Roof Tile

The Period of Nanyue state (203 BC-111 BC)
Residual length: 46 cm/ The widest place: 37 cm

The roof tile is large and thick, from which we can imagine how huge and magnificent the palace of Nanyue state was.
It was unearthed at the Palace Site of Nanyue state in 2002.

"万岁"文字瓦当

南越国时期（公元前 203 ～前 111 年）

直径 16.4 厘米

瓦当在古代多用于宫殿和官署等级别较高的建筑上。秦汉以前，"万岁"一词是欢呼祝颂的代词，用来表达对某人的敬佩或祝福，寓意吉祥。
1997 年南越国宫苑遗址出土。

Eaves Tile with Chinese Characters "*Wan Sui*" (Long Live)

The Period of Nanyue state (203 BC-111 BC)

Diameter: 16.4 cm

Eaves tiles were often used on buildings of higher class, such as palaces and government offices. In Qin and Han Dynasties, "long live" is a word used for congratulations and compliment to express honor or blessing to someone.
It was unearthed at the site of the royal garden of Nanyue state in 1997.

　　1983 年，在广州市象岗山发现南越国第二代王赵眜墓。墓室完全仿效墓主人生前的王宫布局，内出土金、银、铜、铁、陶、石等珍贵文物 1000 多件 (套)，其中 "文帝行玺" 金印、"文帝九年" 铜句鑃等珍贵文物，印证了《史记》《汉书》关于赵佗建立南越国的记载。

　　In 1983, the tomb of the second king of Nanyue state, Zhao Mo, was discovered on Xianggang Mountain in downtown Guangzhou. The layout of the tomb is a complete imitation of the layout of the Nanyue state Palace where he lived before death. More than 1,000 pieces (sets) of precious cultural artifacts made of gold, silver, bronze, iron, pottery, stone and other materials were unearthed. Among them, the gold seal with inscriptions of "*Wen Di Xing Xi*" (the Seal of Emperor Wen) and bronze *GouDiao* with inscriptions of "*Wen Di Jiu Nian*" (the 9th Year of Emperor Wen) are the most precious ones, verifying the historical event of Zhao Tuo's foundation of Nanyue state recorded in *Shi Ji* (The Records of the Grand Historian) and *Han Shu* (the History of the Han Dynasty).

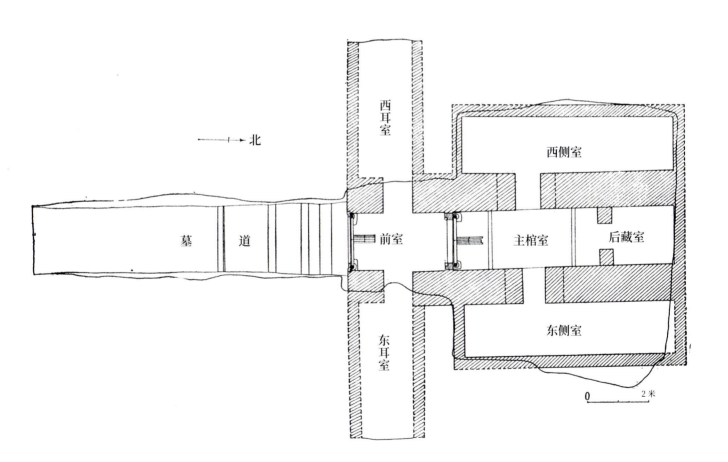

南越文王墓平面图
Plan of the Tomb of King Wen of Nanyue state

后藏室
Rear Storage Chamber

"文帝行玺"龙纽金印

南越国时期（公元前 203 ~ 前 111 年）
印面宽 3.1、通高 1.8 厘米

1983 年南越文王墓出土。

Gold Seal with Dragon Knob with inscriptions of "*Wen Di Xing Xi*"

The Period of Nanyue state (203BC-111BC)
Surface width: 3.1 cm / Height: 1.8 cm

It was unearthed from the tomb of King Wen of Nanyue state in 1983.

"文帝九年" 铜句鑃

南越国时期（公元前 203 ~ 前 111 年）

通高 43.1 厘米

1983 年南越文王墓出土。

Bronze *Goudiao* with inscriptions of "*Wen Di Jiu Nian*"

The Period of Nanyue state(203BC-111BC)

Height: 43.1 cm

It was unearthed from the tomb of King Wen of Nanyue state in 1983.

探索远洋
Exploring the Ocean

　　文献资料记载，越人善舟，习于航海。南越国宫署遗址和南越文王墓以及广州汉墓出土的海外遗物表明，最迟至秦汉之际，南越先民已利用季风沿着海岸线航行，与东南亚和南亚诸国进行交通和贸易往来。

　　考古资料表明，秦汉时期岭南地区的造船技术和规模有了很大的发展，为发展内河航运和沿海海上交通奠定了基础。

　　Literature records show that the Yue people are good at boating and sailing. The Palace Site of Nanyue state, the tomb of Emperor Wen of Nanyue state and overseas items unearthed from tombs of the Han Dynasty in Guangzhou all demonstrate that as late as in Qin and Han Dynasties, ancestors of Nanyue tribes had utilized monsoon to sail along the coastline fot trade and exchange with kingdoms in Southeast Asia and South Asia.

　　Archaeological materials show that in Qin and Han Dynasties, technology and scale of shipbuilding in Lingnan region developed greatly, which laid a foundation for the development of inland waterway and coastal shipping.

铜提筒

南越国时期（公元前 203~前 111 年）
高 40.7、口径 34~35.5、底径 33~33.5 厘米

铜提筒上有四组船纹，描绘了一支大型作战船队凯旋的场景，船体绘出甲板和橹，船内分舱，满载战利品，还画有海鸟和海鱼。这是目前考古发现中规模最大和最为完备的一组海船图形。
1983 年南越文王墓出土。

Bronze Barrel

The period of Nanyue State (203BC-111BC)
Height: 40.7 cm / Mouth Diameter: 34~35.5 cm / Foot Diameter: 33~33.5cm

The bronze barrel is engraved with four groups of ship patterns, depicting the scene of the triumphant return of a large combat fleet. Decks, oars and compartments of the ships can be clearly seen and the ships are fully loaded with trophies and surrounded by seabirds and fishes. This is the largest and the most complete group of ship pattern ever in archaeological discoveries.
It was unearthed from the tomb of King wen of Nanyue state in 1983.

铜鼓

南越国时期（公元前 203~ 前 111 年）
高 36.8、面径 56.4、足径 67.8 厘米

铜鼓鼓身上部饰六组羽人划船纹，船体绘出甲板、橹和隔舱，船头下方绘水鸟和游鱼。

1976 年广西罗泊湾 1 号汉墓出土。

Bronze Drum

The period of Nanyue State (203BC-111BC)
Height: 36.8 cm / Surface Diameter: 56.4cm / Foot Diameter: 67.8cm

---

The bronze drum is decorated with six groups of patterns depicting feathered-men rowing boats on the upper part. Decks, oars and compartments of the ships can be clearly seen while water birds and fishes are depicted below the bows of the ships.

Is was unearthed from tomb1 of the Han Dynasty in Luobowan, Guangxi Province in 1976.

木船模型（复制品）

西汉中期（公元前 110~ 前 33 年）

通长 80.1、通高 20.4、通宽（走道）14.2 厘米

船模两侧有舷板，中部有两舱，前舱方形，四阿顶，后舱长方形，两坡顶，船尾为一小矮舱。
船首有四俑划桨，船尾一俑持桨控制船行方向。这是一艘航行于内河的货船。
1956 年广州西村皇帝岗出土。

Wooden Ship Model (replica)

The Middle Western Han Dynasty (110BC-33BC)
Lenth: 80.1 cm / Height: 20.4 cm / width: 14.2cm

The ship model has plates on both sides and two cabins in the middle. The front cabin is square-shaped
and hip-roofed while the rear cabin is rectangular and slope-roofed. The stern of the ship is a small cabin.
Four figurines are rowing at the front part of the ship, while one figurine is holding oars to control the
direction of the boat at the stern. It is a cargo ship for inland waterways.
It was unearthed in Huangdigang, xicun, Guangzhou in 1956.

南越国宫苑石水池和曲流石渠

　　1995、1997 年考古发现的南越国宫苑遗址主要由一座约 4000 平方米的石水池（蕃池）和长约 160 米的曲流石渠遗迹组成，这是迄今为止我国发现年代最早的宫苑实例。水池和水渠全部用砂岩石材构筑而成，其中池壁和渠底用石板呈密缝铺砌，渠壁用石块错缝垒砌，以及水池当中发现叠石柱遗存等现象，在地中海沿岸地区的古希腊遗址中十分普遍，两者可能存在一定的联系。

　　In 1995 and 1997, the royal garden of Nanyue state was discovered in archaeological excavations. It consists of a stone-walled pond (Pan Chi) of 4,000 square meters and a meandering canal of about 160 meters legnth. It is the earliest royal garden ever discovered in China. The pond and canal built with sandstone, the seamlessly paved pond wall and canal bottom, the staggered joints of stone blocks of the canal walls and the stacked stone columns discovered in the pond are commonly seen in ancient Greek ruins along the Mediterranean coast, indicating there should be certain connections.

石水池池壁
Wall of Stone Pond

石水池中倾倒的叠石柱
Stacked Stone Columns Collapsed in the Stone Pond

曲流石渠渠壁
Wall of Meandering Canal

古希腊提洛岛的叠石柱
Stacked Stone Columns on Delos Island of Ancient Greece

古希腊迈锡尼古城入口
Entrance to the Ancient City of Mycenae in Ancient Greece

古希腊阿波罗神殿（局部）
Temple of Apollo (part) of
Ancient Greece

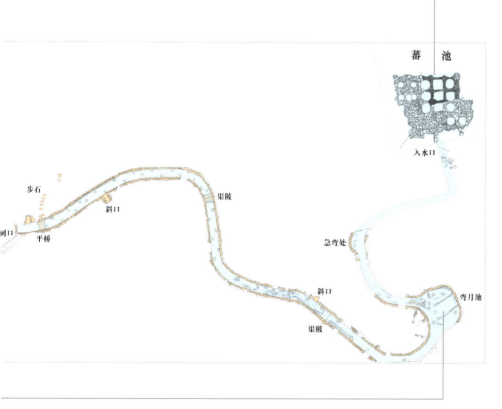

蕃　池

入水口

步石

斜口

渠陂

急弯处

平桥

斜口

弯月池

渠陂

受古希腊、波斯文化艺术影响，公元前 3 世纪至公元前 1 世纪，印度石窟和佛塔等流行使用八角形石柱。南越国宫苑大量使用八角形石柱、八角形石望柱，应是通过海上丝绸之路受到印度文化影响的结果。

Influenced by the culture and art of ancient Greece and Persia, octagonal stone columns were commonly used in Indian grottos and stupas in the 3rd-1st century BC. Octagonal stone columns and pillars widely used in the royal garden of Nanyue state should be influenced by Indian culture, which was brought into China via the Maritime Silk Road.

印度巴贾石窟第 12 窟的八角形石柱
The Octagonal Columns of the 12th Cave of Bhaja Grottos in India

印度桑奇大塔八角形石柱围栏
The Railing of Octagonal Columns of the Great Stupa at Sanchi, India

南越国曲流石渠弯月形水池内的八角形石望柱
Octagonal Pillar of the Crescent Pond in the Meandering Canal of Nanyue State

八角形石柱

南越国时期（公元前 203 ~ 前 111 年）

残长 74、径 24 厘米

1997 年南越国宫苑遗址出土。

Octagonal Stone Column

The Period of Nanyue state (203 BC-111 BC)

Residual Length: 74 cm / Diameter: 24 cm

It was unearthed at the site of the royal garden of Nanyue state in 1997.

八角形石望柱

南越国时期（公元前 203 ~ 前 111 年）
中：残长 45.7、径 12.8 厘米

1995 年南越国宫苑遗址出土。

Octagonal Stone Pillar

The Period of Nanyue state (203 BC-111 BC)
The Middle One: Residual Length: 45.7 cm / Diameter: 12.8 cm

It was unearthed at the site of the royal garden of Nanyue state in 1995.

望柱座石

南越国时期（公元前 203 ~ 前 111 年）
面宽 13.3、底宽 18.4、残长 39 厘米

1995 年南越国宫苑遗址出土。

Stone Pillar Base

The Period of Nanyue state (203 BC-111 BC)
Surface Width: 13.3 cm / Base Width: 18.4 cm / Residual Length: 39 cm

It was unearthed at the site of the royal garden of Nanyue state in 1995.

青釉筒瓦

南越国时期（公元前 203 ~ 前 111 年）
残长 27.5、筒径 15.7 ~ 17 厘米

这是我国目前发现年代最早的釉瓦实例。属钠钾玻璃釉，与公元前 3 世纪印度哈斯蒂纳珀地区的玻璃十分
接近，其制作工艺可能从海外传入。
1995 年南越国宫苑遗址出土。

Celadon Semicircle-shaped Tile

The Period of Nanyue state (203 BC-111 BC)
Residual Length: 27.5 cm / Diameter: 15.7-17 cm

It is the earliest glazed tile ever discovered in China. The sodium-potassium glaze is very similar to the glazed glass in Hastinapur region of India in the 3rd century BC, indicating the technology of the former was possibly overseas.
It was unearthed at the site of the royal garden of Nanyue state in 1995.

玻璃碗

西汉（公元前 206 ~ 公元 25 年）

口径 10.6、壁厚 0.3 厘米

呈深蓝色，半透明。据鉴定属于钠钙玻璃，是公元前 1 世纪地中海罗马
玻璃。

1954 年广州市登峰路横枝岗出土。

Glass Bowl

The Western Han Dynasty (206 BC-25 AD)
Mouth Diameter: 10.6 cm / Thickness: 0.3 cm

The bowl is dark blue and semi-transparent. It is identified as sodium-calcium glass,
a kind of glass made in Mediterranean Roman Empire in 1st Century BC.
It was unearthed in Hengzhigang, Dengfeng Road, Guangzhou in 1954.

串珠

西汉（公元前 206 ~ 公元 25 年）

串珠由水晶、玛瑙、金珠及琉璃珠等组成，各类珠饰共 122 粒。其中一个镂空十二面菱形焊珠小金球，其焊珠工艺源自西亚，而玛瑙则来自印度。这些珠饰应是当时海路贸易的舶来品。2001 年广州市恒福路银行疗养院出土。

String of Beads

The Western Han Dynasty (206 BC-25 AD)

The string of beads is made of crystal, agate, gold and glass and there are 122 beads in total. A diamond-shaped welded hollow gold bead with twelve facets demonstrated the welding technology from West Asia while agate came from India. These beads should be imported through maritime trade.
It was unearthed in the Sanatorium of People's Bank of China on Hengfu Road, Guangzhou in 2001.

自三国至隋唐、南汉国时期，南越国—南汉国宫署遗址一直是历代广州刺史署、都督府、节度使府和南汉王宫等所在。这一时期，因岭南地区社会相对稳定，经济发展，且北方陆路交通常受政局影响通阻无常，朝廷积极发展海上交通贸易，主管广州市舶贸易的地方官员采取积极招徕、自由开放的贸易政策，各国番舶纷至沓来，每年到达广州的商舶激增，至唐朝时达到鼎盛，使广州成为当时东方第一大港。

From the Three Kingdoms Period to Sui and Tang Dynasties as well as the following Nanhan State Period, the Palace site of Nanyue and Nanyue states was also the location of *Ci Shi Shu* (Prefect Office), *Du Du Fu* (Governor Office), *Jie Du Shi Fu* (Regional Commander Office) and the Palace of Nanhan state over the time. During these periods, the court encouraged maritime trade in view of the social stability and economic development in Lingnan region and the interrupted land transportation in north China under the influence of the political situation. Local maritime trade supervisors adopted favorable policies to encourage open and free trade. Foreign ships rolled in to Guangzhou, reaching a peak in the Tang Dynasty and making the city the largest port in the Orient.

积极南拓

The Expansion to the South

　　三国时期，交州刺史步骘将州治迁至番禺，在南越王宫遗址之上筑立城郭，其后孙权又分交州置广州，加强了广州在政治、经济上的地位。随着造船业和航海技术的进步，孙吴时开辟一条自广州启航、经南海直达东南亚各国的航线，海上交往日益频繁。晋、南朝时期，经海上丝绸之路来到广州的僧侣、外国使节、商人络绎不绝，进一步促进了东西方文化、宗教、技术的交流与融合。

　　In the Three Kingdoms Period, Bu Zhi, prefect of Jiaozhou (Jiao Province), moved the capital of the Province to Panyu and built city walls on the ruins of Nanyue state Palace. Later, Sun Quan, King of the Wu State, separated Guangzhou (Guang Province) from Jiaozhou and improved the political and economic status of Guangzhou. With the development of shipbuilding industry and the progress of sailing technology, a maritime route starting from Guangzhou, via South China Sea and reaching multiple countries in Southeast Asia was formed during the Wu state period and overseas exchange became increasingly frequent. In the Jin Dynasty and the Southern Dynasties, there were many monks, foreign envoys and merchants arriving in Guangzhou through the Maritime Silk Road, further promoting the exchange and integration of culture, religion and technology between the east and the west.

据《三国志·吴书》记载，孙吴黄武五年（226年）分交州置广州，这是"广州"得名之始，为广州此后的发展奠定了政治基础。

According to the *Book of Wu* in the *Records of the Three Kingdoms*, Guangzhou was separated from Jiaozhou in the 5th year of Huangwu Period (226 AD) of the Wu State. This is how Guangzhou received its name and laid a political foundation for its future development.

三国时期交州和广州分治示意图
Map of the Separation of Jiaozhou and Guangzhou in the Three Kingdoms Period

《三国志·吴书·吕岱传》
Biography of Lv Dai, Book of Wu, Records of the Three Kingdoms

　　文献记载，三国孙权时派使者从广州出发，经海南岛以东和西沙群岛海域直航出使林邑、扶南（今越南中南部）等国。随着航海技术的提高，广州逐渐成为最重要的海外贸易港口。

　　It is recorded in historical literature that during the reign of Sun Quan in the Three Kingdoms Period, envoys were sent to start sail from Guangzhou, via the sea east of Hainan Island and the Xisha Islands, to Linyi (Lâm Âp in Vietnamese, a kingdom in what is today central Vietnam) and Funan (central and south Vietnam). With the improvement of navigation technology, Guangzhou was gradually shaped into the most important port for overseas trade.

青瓷六耳罐

三国时期（公元 220 ～ 265 年）
口径 8.6、高 22 厘米

表面施青釉，造型精美别致。
1997 年南越国宫署遗址出土。

Six-earred Celadon Jar

The Three Kingdoms Period (220-265 AD)
Mouth Diameter: 8.6 cm / Height: 22 cm

It is celadon-glazed and in an exquisite and unique shape.
It was unearthed at the Palace Site of Nanyue state in 1997.

陶四耳罐

三国时期（公元 220 ～ 265 年）

口径 13.2、高 19.2 厘米

1997 年南越国宫署遗址出土。

Four-earred Pottery Jar

The Three Kingdoms Period (220-265 AD)
Mouth Diameter: 13.2cm / Height: 19.2 cm

It was unearthed at the Palace Site of Nanyue state in 1997.

陶双耳罐

三国时期（公元 220 ~ 265 年）

口径 3.0、高 5.2 厘米

1997 年南越国宫署遗址出土。

Double-earred Pottery Jar

The Three Kingdoms Period (220-265 AD)
Mouth Diameter: 3.0 cm / Height: 5.2 cm

It was unearthed at the Palace Site of Nanyue state in 1997.

陶双耳壶

三国时期（公元 220 ~ 265 年）

口径 2.4、高 7.6 厘米

1997 年南越国宫署遗址出土。

Double-earred Pottery Jar

The Three Kingdoms Period (220-265 AD)
Mouth Diameter: 2.4 cm / Height: 7.6 cm

It was unearthed at the Palace Site of Nanyue state in 1997.

　　文献记载，晋、南朝时期，广州海外珍宝聚集，一些主管市舶贸易的官员借机敛财，但吴隐之、萧劢等为官清廉，秋毫不犯，使来广州贸易的番舶大增，促进了广州海外贸易蓬勃发展。

　　It is recorded that during the period of the Jin Dynasty and the Southern Dynasties, Guangzhou was where overseas treasures were imported and distributed and some maritime trade supervisors abused their power for personal interests. Wu Yinzhi and Xiao Mai, on the contrary, were upright and remained uncorrupted. Under their governance, overseas trade increased and developed notably in Guangzhou.

《南史·萧劢传》
Biography of Xiao Mai, History of the Southern Dynasties

石门贪泉
Tan Quan (The Spring of Greed) in Shimen

在广州北郊石门有泉名贪泉，因传说人饮其水起贪心而得名。东晋广州刺史吴隐之上任路过此地酌泉而饮，还赋诗"古人云此水，一饮怀千金。试使夷齐饮，终当不移心"以喻其志。他主政广州期间，为官清廉，维护番商利益，使广州的海外贸易蓬勃发展。

In Shimen, the northern suburb of Guangzhou, there is a spring named *Tan Quan* (the Spring of Greed). It was said that when people drank the water from the spring, they would become greedy. When Wu Yinzhi, the Prefect of Guangzhou in the Eastern Jin Dynasty, passed by the spring in his way to take up his post, he drank water from the spring and wrote a poem: *A legend says a sip from this spring, makes people be greedy for money. Try not to test it with Bo Yi and Shu Qi, they would never give up their integrity*. When he governed Guangzhou, he was incorruptible and defended the interests of the foreign merchants, making Guangzhou's overseas trade flourish.

吴隐之饮贪泉水
Wu Yinzhi Drinking Water from the Spring of Greed

三国时期，岭南为东吴所辖。两晋、南北朝时期，中原战乱频仍，岭南相对稳定，人民大量南迁，此时广州在经济、文化方面取得了很大发展。南越国宫署遗址内发现有南朝时期的官署遗迹，应是兼管海外贸易的广州刺史署所在地。

During the Three Kingdoms Period, Lingnan region was within the territory of the Wu State. During the Western and Eastern Jin Dynasties as well as the Northern and Southern Dynasties, people moved southward because wars frequently broke out in the Central Plains region while the Lingnan region was relatively stable. The immigration helped Guangzhou achieve great development in economy and culture. Ruins of government office of the Southern Dynasties found in the Palace Site of Nanyue state should be *Ci Shi Shu* (Prefect Office) which was in charge of overseas trade.

南朝官署建筑遗迹
The Building Remains of the Government office of the Southern Dynasties

玻璃料珠

东晋（公元 317 ~ 420 年）

外径 0.36 厘米

又名费昂斯珠子，来自南亚或东南亚地区。魏晋南北朝时期，玻璃制品造型美观，但数量稀少，大多为舶来品，多与玻璃管串成饰物。

2000 年南越国宫署遗址出土。

Glass Bead

The Eastern Jin Dynasty (317-420 AD)
Outer Diameter: 0.36 cm

It is also named Faience bead and came from South Asia or Southeast Asia. Glass vessels during the Wei and Jin Dynasties as well as the Northern and Southern Dynasties were found beautifully designed but very rare and mostly imported. Glass beads and glass tubes were often made into accessories.

It was unearthed at the Palace Site of Nanyue state in 2000.

玻璃料珠

南朝（公元 420 ~ 589 年）

外径 0.5~0.6 厘米

1997 年南越国宫署遗址出土。

Glass bead

The Southern Dynasties (420-589 AD)
Outer Diameter: 0.5-0.6 cm

It was unearthed at the Palace Site of Nanyue state in 1997.

莲花纹瓦当

东晋（公元 317 ~ 420 年）
当径 15.8 厘米

莲花是佛教的圣物，代表清净庄严，是佛国净土的象征。自佛教从海上丝绸之路传入中国后，以莲花为装饰的图案广泛应用于建筑、艺术和生活器物等方面。1997 年南越国宫署遗址出土。

Eaves Tile with Lotus Pattern

The Eastern Jin Dynasty (317-420 AD)
Diameter: 15.8 cm

Lotus is sacred to Buddhism, representing divine beauty and purity. It is the symbol of Sukhavati which means pure land of a Buddha. Since the introduction of Buddhism into China via the Maritime Silk Road, the pattern of lotus flower is widely used in architecture, art and utensils as one of the major decorative patterns.
It was unearthed at the Palace Site of Nanyue state in 1997.

莲花纹瓦当

南朝（公元 420 ~ 589 年）

当径 14 厘米

1997 年南越国宫署遗址出土。

Eaves Tile with Lotus Pattern

The Southern Dynasties (420-589 AD)
Diameter: 14 cm

It was unearthed at the Palace Site of Nanyue state in 1997.

莲花纹砖

南朝（公元 420 ~ 589 年）
残长 13.4、宽 16、厚 3.2 厘米

1997 年南越国宫署遗址出土。

Brick with Lotus Pattern

The Southern Dynasties (420-589 AD)
Residual Length: 13.4 cm / Width: 16 cm / Thickness: 3.2 cm

It was unearthed at the Palace Site of Nanyue state in 1997.

市舶始开
The Beginning of the official Maritime Trade

随着海上交通贸易的迅速发展，隋文帝于开皇十四年（594 年）在广州建造了南海神庙祭祀海神，以祈求海贸平安。唐开元二年（714 年）在广州首设市舶使，专门负责管理番货海贸，又在城西外国人聚居地设置"番坊"，招徕番商。唐代对外通道多达七条，其中"广州通海夷道"是当时世界上航线最长的通道，最远已达红海和非洲东海岸，广州成为当时中国乃至世界上最大的海上贸易港口。南越国宫署遗址是隋唐时期管理海外贸易事务的广州刺史署和节度使府的所在地。

With the rapid development of maritime transportation and overseas trade, in the 14th year of Kaihuang Period of Emperor Wen of the Sui Dynasty (594 AD), the God Temple of the South Sea was built to worship the God of Sea and to pray for peace of overseas trade. In the 2nd year of Kaiyuan Period of the Tang Dynasty (714 AD), the first *Shi Bo Shi* (Maritime Trade Supervisor) was sent in Guangzhou, overseeing foreign commodities and overseas trade. In the western suburb of Guangzhou where most foreigners chose to live, *Fan Fang* (Foreigners'Community) was established to attract foreign merchants. In the Tang Dynasty, there were seven maritime routes and *Guangzhou Tong Hai Yi Dao* (the Guangzhou Overseas Trade Route) was the longest one, which reached the Red Sea and the east coast of Africa. Guangzhou was the largest maritime trade port in China and even in the world at that time. The Palace Site of Nanyue state was also the location of Guangzhou *Ci Shi Shu* (Prefect Office) and *Jie Du Shi Fu* (Regional Commander Office) which were in charge of overseas trade affairs in Sui and Tang Dynasties.

唐代的市舶管理

晋南朝至唐初，市舶事务多由刺史、太守等地方长官管理。为了适应海外贸易的快速发展，最迟至唐开元二年（714年）在广州首设市舶使，与节度使共同管理海外贸易。节度使主要职掌对外贸易和外商司法管理等具体事务。市舶使则由监军兼任，多由宦官充当，代表皇权，主要负责收市供奉和监察市舶事务。

Official Maritime Trade in the Tang Dynasty

From the Jin Dynasty and the Southern Dynasties to early Tang Dynasty, maritime trade affairs were managed by prefects, governors and other local officers. In order to adapt to the rapid development of overseas trade, the first *Shi Bo Shi* (Maritime Trade Supervisor) was sent in Guangzhou in the 2nd year of Kaiyuan Period in the Tang Dynasty (714 AD) to supervise overseas trade together with *Jie Du Shi* (Regional Commander). *Jie Du Shi* was responsible for specific matters of foreign trade and foreigner-related judicial affairs while the post of *Shi Bo Shi* was usually assumed concurrently by *Jian Jun* (Army Overseers), who were mostly eunuchs sent by the emperor as representatives of the imperial authority and mainly responsible for collecting tributes and supervising maritime trade affairs.

唐代海外贸易管理连环画
Comics about Overseas Trade Administration in the Tang Dynasty

1. 奏报。番舶进港后，地方要上报朝廷。
1.Reporting to the emperor. After foreign ships arrived at the port, the local authorities should report the issue to the imperial court.

2. 检阅。官员对船货进行检验。
2.Inspection. The officials inspected the ship and freight.

3. 款待。设"阅货宴"招待远道而来的客商。
3.Reception and entertaining. A banquant was arranged to showcase the commodities and entertain the merchants travelling from afar.

4. 纳舶脚。即收取关税。
4.Tax payment. Duties were collected.

5. 收市。高价收买珍贵的物品进奉朝廷。
5.Acquisition from the market. Precious goods were bought at high price and presented to the imperial court.

6. 作法。制定有关番舶管理法令。
6.Making laws. Laws and regulations on administration of foreign ships were formulated.

1989 年，西安市西郊出土了三笏银铤，这是波斯商人伊娑郝于唐大历末、建中初年客死广州时留下的遗产。其遗产三个月内无亲属认领，被广州官府没收，由负责广州外贸管理的岭南节度使张伯仪和市舶使刘楚江进献给朝廷。这与 9 世纪阿拉伯商人撰写的《中国印度见闻录》中的记载相一致。这些银铤的出土，证实唐代海外贸易是由节度使和市舶使共同管理。

In 1989, three silver bars were unearthed in western suburb of Xi'an. They were the legacy of a Persian merchant, Ishaq, who died in Guangzhou at the end of Dali Period and the beginning of Jianzhong Period in the Tang Dynasty. As the legacy was not claimed within three months, it was confiscated by the government of Guangzhou and paid to the court as a tribute by *Jie Du Shi* (Regional Commander) Zhang Boyi and *Shi Bo Shi* (Maritime Trade Supervisor) Liu Chujiang. The story was in line with the records in the *Ancient Accounts of India and China* written by an Arabian merchant in the 9th century. These silver bars are evidence confirming the assumption that in the Tang Dynasty, overseas trade was jointly supervised by *Jie Du Shi* and *Shi Bo Shi*.

《中国印度见闻录》
Ancient Accounts of India and China

波斯伊娑郝银铤拓片
Rubbing of the Silver Bar of Persian Merchant Ishaq

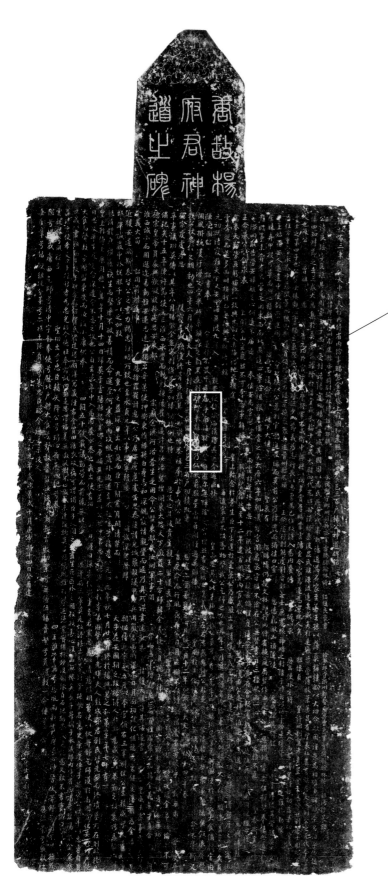

《杨良瑶神道碑》碑文拓本及局部
Rubbing and part of the inscription on *the Gravestone of Yang Liangyao*

杨良瑶（736~806 年），陕西泾阳人。唐贞
元元年（785 年）四月，受命由广州经海路出使黑
衣大食（西亚），成为我国第一位航海抵波斯湾沿
岸的外交使节，早于传统所认为的"下西洋第一人"
郑和。

Yang Liangyao (736-806 AD) was born in
Jinyang, Shaanxi. In April of the 1st year of Zhenyuan
Period (785 AD), he was sent on a diplomatic
mission to travel by sea via Guangzhou to Abbasid
Caliphate (commonly known as Hei Yi Da Shi or The
Black-robed Tazi in the Tang Dynasty, Tazi being the
Persian word for Arab) in West Asia. Yang was the first
Chinese envoy who ever reached the shore of Persian
Gulf and his mission was much earlier than Zhen He,
who was misunderstood as the first person who ever
travelled to the West Seas.

唐代可考市舶使名单

姓 名	时 间	地 点	身 份	资料出处
周庆立	开元二年	广州	本官：右威卫中郎将	《旧唐书·玄宗纪》
韦光闰	开元十年后至天宝初	广州	本官：内府局丞	《内给事谏议大夫韦公神道碑》[1]《韦光闰妻宋氏墓志》[2]
缺名（中人之市舶使）	天宝八载	广州	宦官	《新唐书·卢奂传》
吕太一	广德元年	广州	宦官	《旧唐书·代宗纪》
孙荣义	大历中	广州	宦官（监军兼任）	《权德舆诗文集》
刘楚江	大历末至建中初	广州	宦官（岭南监军、内侍省内给事）	《西安西郊发现唐银锭》[3]
许遂振	元和五年	广州	宦官（监军兼任）	《李文公集》
缺名	开成元年	广州	宦官（监军兼任）	《旧唐书·卢钧传》
李敬实	大中四年	广州	宦官（都监兼任）	《李敬实墓志》[4]
缺名	唐末	广州	宦官	《中国印度见闻录》

[1] 《内给事谏议大夫韦公神道碑》出处：《全唐文》，卷三七一，于肃静作。

[2] 《韦光闰妻宋氏墓志》出处：周绍良、赵超编《唐代墓志汇编续集》，乾元〇〇四，上海古籍出版社，2001 年。

[3] 《西安西郊发现唐银锭》出处：王长启、高曼《西安西郊发现唐银锭》，《中国钱币》2001 年第 1 期。

[4] 《李敬实墓志》出处：《唐代墓志汇编续集》，大中〇七八。

List of *Shi Bo Shi* (Maritime Trade Supervisors) in the Tang Dynasty

Name	Time	Location	Title	Source
Zhou Qingli	The 2nd year of Kaiyuan Period	Guangzhou	You Wei Wei Zhong LangJiang (Commander of the Palace Guard Squad)	*Biography of Emperor Xuanzong, Old Book of Tang*
Wei Guangrun	The 10th year of Kaiyuan Period to early Tianbao Period	Guangzhou	Nei Fu Ju Cheng (Assistant Director of Imperial Storehouse)	*Gravestone on the Sacred Way of Wei Guangrun, the Imperial Advisor of Inner Court* *Epigraph of Song Shi, Wife of Wei Guangrun*
Anonymous (The Shi Bo Shi was an eunuch)	The 8th year of Tianbao Period	Guangzhou	Eunuch	*Biography of Lu Huan, New Book of Tang*
Lv Taiyi	The 1st year of Guangde Period	Guangzhou	Eunuch	*Biography of Daizong, Old Book of Tang*
Sun Rongyi	Middle of Dali Period	Guangzhou	Eunuch (concurrently Army Overseer)	*Collection of Essays and Poems of Quan Deyu*
Liu Chujiang	Late Dali Period to early Jianzhong Period	Guangzhou	Eunuch (concurrently Army Overseer of Lingnan and Inner Court Officer of Imperial Office Bureau)	*Silver Ingot Discovered in Western Suburb of Xi'an*
Xu Suizhen	The 5th year of Yuanhe Period	Guangzhou	Eunuch (concurrently Army Overseer)	*Collection of Li Wen Gong* (Wen Gong is the posthumous title of Li Ao [772–841 AD], philosopher and prose writer of the Tang Dynasty)
Anonymous	The 1st year of Kaicheng Period	Guangzhou	Eunuch (concurrently Army Overseer)	*Biography of Lu Jun, Old Book of Tang*
Li Jingshi	The 4th year of Dazhong Period	Guangzhou	Eunuch (concurrently Army Overseer)	*Epigraph of Li Jingshi*
Anonymous	Late Tang Dynasty	Guangzhou	Eunuch	*Ancient Accounts of India and China*

孔戣与南海神庙
Kong Kui and the God Temple of the South Sea

　　孔戣（753~825 年），字君严，是孔子三十八代孙。唐宪宗对宰相拟定的岭南节度使人选不满意，亲自选定孔戣。孙戣一到任就免去了属下州县所欠的大笔钱粮，为民减负；又严禁官员收取番商礼品，破除外商死后三个月内无人认领即予没收等不合理法令，大力改善外商环境，促进外贸发展。

　　Kong Kui (753-825 AD), courtesy name Junyan, was the 38th-generation-descendant of Confucius. Emperor Xianzong of the Tang Dynasty was not satisfied with the proposed Lingnan *Jie Du Shi* (Lingnan Regional Commander) selected by the Prime Minister and appointed Kong Kui instead. As soon as kongkui assumed the post, he exempted provinces and counties under his governance from a large amount of tax in currency and in grain. He also announced that government officers were forbidden to accept gifts from foreign merchants and withdrew the unreasonable decree to confiscate legacies of foreign merchants if they were not claimed within three months after the owners' death. The environment for foreign trade was greatly improved with his efforts.

韩愈撰《南海神广利王庙碑》拓本
Rubbing of the Inscription on *the Stele of the Temple of Dragon King of South Sea* written by Han Yu

《南海神广利王庙碑》记载了孔戣多次到南海神庙祭祀南海神、扩大庙宫以及在广州的德政。

有关航海技术、航运的"海事"一词，最早见于此碑。

The inscription on *the Stele of the Temple of Dragon King of South Sea* recorded Kong Kui's multiple visits to the God Temple of the South Sea and sacrifices to the God of the South Sea, as well as his orders to expand the Temple and his benevolent governance in Guangzhou.

The word *Hai Shi* (literally: maritime affairs) occurred for the first time on this stele.

路嗣恭（约 710~780 年），字懿范，京兆郡三原县（今陕西三原县东北三十里）人。唐大历八年（773 年）任岭南节度使，平定哥舒晃叛乱后向唐代宗进献一个直径九寸的外国玻璃盘，皇上以为是天下至宝。后宰相元载因贪污获罪，代宗派人查抄元载的家时，搜出路嗣恭贿赂元载的一个外国玻璃盘，直径达一尺，令代宗耿耿于怀。路嗣恭在广州得到的玻璃盘，应该是通过海上贸易，从西亚进口的伊斯兰玻璃。

Lu Sigong (around 710-780 AD), courtesy name Yifan, was born in Sanyuan County of Jingzhao Prefecture (15 kilometers northeast from present Sanyuan County in Shaanxi Province). He assumed the post of Lingnan *Jie Du Shi* (Lingnan Regional Commander) in the 8th year of Dali Period (773 AD) of the Tang Dynasty and presented tribute to Emperor Daizong with a foreign glass dish of 9 *Cun* in diameter (around 27.6 cm, 1 *Cun* was around 3.07 cm in the Tang Dynasty) after quelling the rebellion of Geshu Huang, which the Emperor believed to be the most precious treasure at the time. Later when Yuan Zai, the prime minister, was imprisoned because of bribery and his property was confiscated, Emperor Daizong was very unhappy to find a larger dish of same kind of 10 *Cun* in diameter (around 30.7 cm) in his possessions which was the bribe from Lu Sigong. The glass dishes that Lu Sigong obtained in Guangzhou were believed to be Islamic glass wares imported from West Asia through maritime trade.

路嗣恭画像
Portrait of Lu Sigong

伊斯兰蓝色玻璃盘

公元 9 世纪

口径 20 厘米

1987 年陕西西安法门寺出土。

Blue Islamic Glass Dish

The 9th century AD

Mouth Diameter: 20 cm

It was unearthed at Famen Temple，Xi'an，Shaanxi Province.

伊斯兰黄色玻璃盘

公元 9 世纪

口径 14 厘米

1987 年陕西西安法门寺出土。

Yellow Islamic Glass Dish

The 9th century AD

Mouth Diameter: 14 cm

It was unearthed at Famen Temple，Xi'an，Shaanxi Province.

（以上两图资料来自：陕西省考古研究院等编著的《法门寺考古发掘报告》，文物出版社，2007 年。*Report of Archaeological Excavation at Famen Temple*, Cultural Relics Press, 2007.）

唐代建筑基址
Site Bases of Buildings in the Tang Dynasty

唐代铺砖走道
Paved Walkway in the Tang Dynasty

玻璃杯

公元 8 ~ 9 世纪
口径 7.7 厘米

做工精细，胎体极薄。从造型和化学成分分析，是从西亚地区进口的伊斯兰玻璃。
1997 年南越国宫署遗址出土。

Glass Cup

The 8th to 9th century AD
Mouth Diameter: 7.7 cm

It was finely made with very thin glass. Judged from the design and chemical elements, it was Islamic glass imported from West Asia.
It was unearthed at the Palace Site of Nanyue state in 1997.

　　黑石号是 1998 年在印度尼西亚勿里洞岛海域发现的一艘阿拉伯沉船，该船由广州经东南亚前往波斯湾途中沉没。船上装载唐代中国瓷器约 6.7 万件，其中长沙窑瓷器就达 5 万件。长沙窑是唐代最重要的窑址之一，位于今湖南长沙北郊，又名铜官窑。随着唐代制瓷业的发展及海上交通的开发，长沙窑瓷器不但行销国内，更远销海外。

　　Batu Hitam Shipwreck is the wreck of an Arabian dhow discovered off the coast of Belitung Island, Indonesia. It sank on route from Guangzhou to the Persian Gulf via Southeast Asia. The dhow carried 67,000 porcelain wares of the Tang Dynasty, among which, 50,000 were wares of Changsha kiln. Changsha kiln is one of the most important kilns in the Tang Dynasty. It was located in the northern suburb of modern day Changsha, Hunan and also known as Tongguan kiln. With the development of ceramic industry of the Tang Dynasty and the maritime transportation, wares of Changsha kiln were sold not only at domestic market, but also in overseas market.

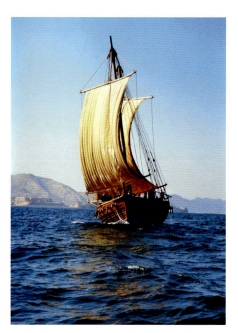

复原的黑石号帆船
Replica of Batu Hitam Shipwreck

1994 年广州市德政中路唐代码头遗址出土的长沙窑瓷片
Fragments of wares of Changsha kiln unearthed from the Pier Ruins of the Tang Dynasty on Dezheng Middle Road, Guangzhou in 1994

黑石号沉船出土的长沙窑彩绘纹盘
Dishes with Painted Pattern from Changsha kiln Found from the Batu Hitam Shipwreck

1994 年，在广州市德政中路发掘出唐代码头遗址，四周堆满大量的长沙窑等地生产的瓷器残片，说明广州是唐代陶瓷的重要出口港。

In 1994, pier ruins of the Tang Dynasty were discovered in Dezheng Middle Road, Guangzhou, together with a large number of fragments of wares of Changsha kiln as well as other kilns, showing that Guangzhou was an important port for ceramics export in the Tang Dynasty.

唐代码头遗址
The Pier Ruins of the Tang Dynasty

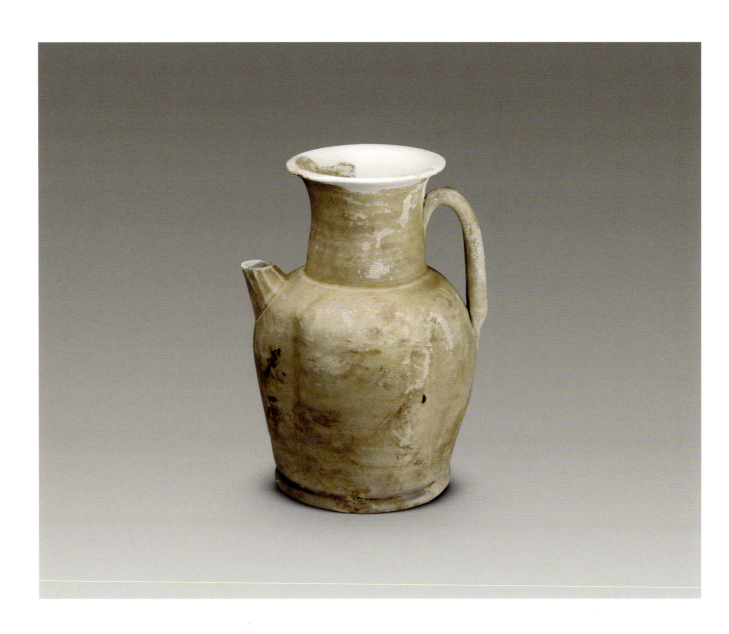

长沙窑青瓷褐彩诗文执壶

唐代（公元 618 ~ 907 年）
口径 8.7、高 17.8 厘米

流嘴下腹部用褐彩书写"忍辱成端政"五个字。
2005 年南越国宫署遗址出土。

Celadon Ewer with Brown-colored Calligraphy of Changsha Kiln

The Tang Dynasty (618-907 AD)
Mouth Diameter: 8.7 cm / Height: 17.8 cm

Characters "*Ren Ru Cheng Duan Zheng*" are written in brown color on the lower part
of the ewer.
It was unearthed at the Palace Site of Nanyue state in 2005.

长沙窑青瓷褐彩狗

唐代（公元 618 ～ 907 年）

长 6.4、高 5.0 厘米

长沙窑除生产大量壶、碗、罐、瓶等生活用器外，还生产鸟、兽、人物俑，极富生活气息。
2005 年南越国宫署遗址出土。

Brown-colored Celadon Dog of Changsha Kiln

The Tang Dynasty (618-907 AD)

Length: 6.4 cm / Height: 5.0 cm

In addition to a large number of daily utensils, such as kettles, bowls, jars and bottles, Changsha Kiln also
produced bird, animal and human figurines that reflected the daily life of that time.
It was unearthed at the Palace Site of Nanyue state in 2005.

象牙人头雕像

唐代（公元 618 ～ 907 年）

通高 3 厘米

为半身像，高鼻，深目，卷发，此为一外国人头形象。
2000 年南越国宫署遗址出土。

Ivory Head Statue

The Tang Dynasty (618-907 AD)

Height: 3 cm

This is a bust of a foreigner with a high nose, deep eyes and curly hair. It was unearthed at the Palace Site of Nanyue State in 2000.

牛角

唐代（公元 618 ～ 907 年）

长 46.0、最宽 13.5 厘米

犀牛角是海上丝绸之路热销宝物之一，因供不应求，一些不法商人常用水牛角冒充。
2007 年南越国宫署遗址出土。

Buffalo Horn

The Tang Dynasty (618-907 AD)

Length: 46.0 cm / Maximum Width: 13.5 cm

Rhino horns were one of the most precious commodities of the Maritime Silk Road and they were often in short supply. Some merchants passed buffalo horns off as rhino horns for high profit. It was unearthed at the Palace Site of Nanyue state in 2007.

以海强国

Improving State Strength with the Maritime Trade

公元 10 世纪初，唐代灭亡，中国进入五代十国时期。位于岭南的南汉国极力发展海上交通贸易，一时间海上私人交易、官方贸易活动非常活跃，南汉国凭借海上丝绸之路的地缘优势快速发展。近年来考古发现的南汉宫殿及文物，极显雄伟与奢华，与文献中关于南汉皇帝悉聚南海珍宝营建宫室的记载相符。

At the beginning of the 10th century AD, the Tang Dynasty ended and was replaced by the Five Dynasties and Ten States Period. The Nanhan state in Lingnan region introduced the national policy to develop maritime transportation and trade. Non-governmental and governmental maritime trade had great momentum at the time. The Nanhan state developed quickly with its geographic advantage of the Maritime Silk Road. The magnificence and extravagance of the Nanhan state Palace and cultural artifacts unearthed in latest archaeological discoveries are in line with the historical records about how the kings of the Nanhan state collected numerous treasures from the South Sea to build their palace.

南汉国二号宫殿前殿台基
The Raised Platform of the Front Hall of No.2 Palace of the Nanhan State

南汉国二号宫殿北庭院铺蝴蝶纹、牡丹纹砖地面
Bricks with Butterfly Pattern and Peony Pattern Paved in the Northern Courtyard of No.2 Palace of the Nanhan State

蝴蝶纹方砖

南汉国时期（公元 917 ~ 971 年）

边长 35 厘米

宫殿庭院地面铺地砖。砖面模印四只展翅飞舞的蝴蝶，四角饰牡丹纹。牡丹象征富贵，蝴蝶与"叠"字谐音，寓意"富贵叠来"。反映南汉凭借海上丝绸之路优势国家富足。

2009 年南越国宫署遗址出土。

Square Brick with Butterfly Pattern

The Period of Nanhan state (917-971 AD)
Side Length: 35 cm

The brick was used to pave the ground of the palace courtyard. Pattern of four flying butterflies was stamped on the brick with peony patterns on four corners. Peony is the symbol for wealth and honor while butterfly is a homonym of *Die* (repetition) in Chinese language, which together mean ceaseless wealth and honor. It reflects the wealth of the Nanhan state because of overseas trade on the Maritime Silk Road.

It was unearthed at the Palace Site of Nanyue state in 2009.

波斯蓝釉陶片

公元 10 世纪

古代波斯素以制陶著称，南汉国王宫遗址出土的波斯蓝釉陶片数量较多，说明南汉与波斯贸易往来密切。1997 年南越国宫署遗址出土。

Blue-glazed Persian Potsherds

The 10th century AD

Ancient Persian Empire was well known for pottery making. Many blue-glazed Persian potsherds were discovered at the Palace Site of Nanhan state , which reflects that the Nanhan state had close trade relationships with Persian.
It was unearthed at the Palace Site of Nanyue state in 1997.

贴塑弦纹绿石釉四耳大陶罐

公元 9 世纪
高 74.5 厘米

福建闽越国刘华墓出土。

Four-earred Green Glazed Pottery Jar with Pasted String Pattern

The 9th century AD
Height: 74.5cm

It was unearthed from Liuhua Tomb of Minyue state in Fujian Province.

玻璃瓶

公元 10 世纪
口径 5.2、高 12 厘米

康陵是南汉开国皇帝刘岩的陵墓。墓内出土了一百多片玻璃残片，
其中一件玻璃瓶可复原，经分析为伊斯兰玻璃。
2003 年南汉康陵出土。

Glass Vase

The 10th century AD
Mouth Diameter: 5.2 cm / Height: 12 cm

Kangling Mausoleum is the tomb of Liu Yan, the founding king of Nanhan
state. More than 100 pieces of glass fragments were unearthed in the tomb. One
of the bottles was restored and analyzed to be Islamic glass.
It was unearthed from Kangling Mausoleum of Nanhan state in 2003.

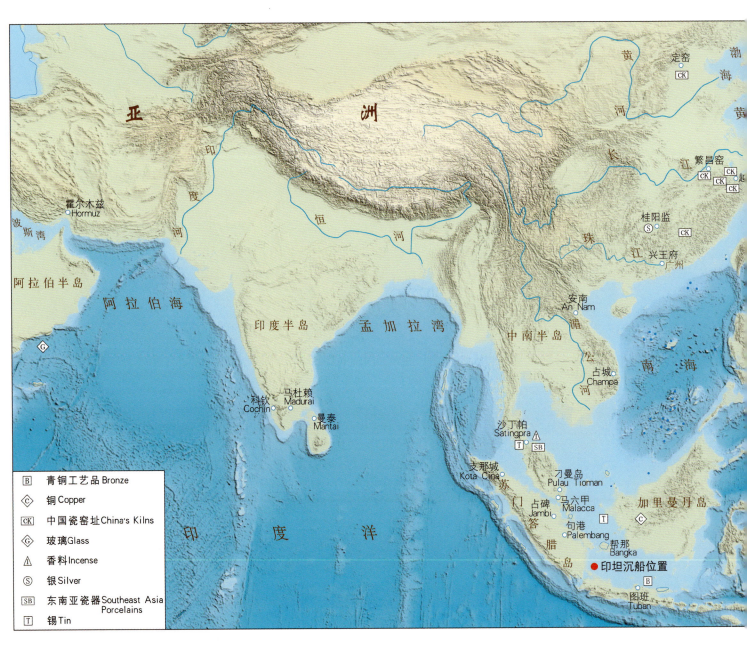

印坦沉船货物出处示意图（据杜思德、思鉴《沉船遗宝：一艘十世纪沉船上的中国银锭》
地图二改绘，《唐研究》第十卷，北京大学出版社，2004 年）
Map of the Origin of the Cargo Found on the Intan Shipwreck in the Java Sea（Redrawn according
to Map Ⅱ in *The Lost Treasure of the Shipwreck: Chinese Silver Ingots on a Ten-Century Shipwreck*
written by Du Side and Si Jian, Study of the Tang, Vol.10, Peking University Press, 2004）

1997 年，在印尼雅加达以北约 150 千米的印坦油田海域，打捞出一艘于公元 920 ～ 960 年间从广州贸易归航的东南亚籍商船。原船装载有大量货物，其中有 7 千多件珍贵的中国陶瓷和南汉银铤、"乾亨重宝"铅钱等文物。

印坦沉船共清理出 80 枚银铤，总重量约 70 千克。部分铸有"桂阳监"三字，部分外套银封刻有盐税（或银务）上色银若干拾两若干钱专知官等字样。同船伴出 100 多枚南汉国的"乾亨重宝"铅钱。据相关研究，可确认这批银铤为南汉国铸造，时间在 951~964 年。以此为凭，可确认印坦沉船是以南汉作为贸易对象，而南汉以桂阳监制的银铤成批购买海外商货。由此可见，南汉时广州实乃中西海上交通贸易之重要港口。

In 1997, a shipwreck was found in the Java Sea near Intan Oil Platform, 150 km north of Jakarta, the capital of Indonesia. It was a merchant ship from Southeast Asia heading back home from Guangzhou around 920-960 AD. The ship was fully loaded with a large number of commodities, including more than seven thousand of very precious Chinese ceramics, silver bars and *"Qian Heng Zhong Bao* (currency of the Qianheng Period)" lead coins from the Nanhan state.

There were 80 silver bars on the wreck, the weight of which is around 70 kg in total. Some of them were inscribed with three Chinese characters of *Gui Yang Jian* (Guiyang Supervisor of Mining and Coinage) and some others were with inscriptions of *Yan Shui* (Salt Tax) or *Yin Wu* (Coinage) *Shang Se Yin XX Shi Liang XX Qian Zhuan Zhi Guan* (Fine Silver of XX Shiliang [weight around 312.5g]. XX Qian [weight around 3.13g]). More than 100 *"Qian Heng Zhong Bao"* lead coins of the Nanhan state were found on the wreck. According to relevant studies, these silver bars were cast by the Nanhan state government around 951-964 AD. We are almost sure on this basis that Intan shipwreck must be trading with the Nanhan state and the Nanhan state used silver bars cast by Guiyang Supervisor of Mining and Coinage to purchase overseas commodities. It shows that Guangzhou was an important port for maritime transportation and trade between China and the West in the period of Nanhan state.

铅锭

南汉国时期（公元 917 ~ 971 年）

长 24.5、宽 10.0、厚 4.1 厘米，重 6.3 千克

正面和侧面刻有"春州铅十斤"等铭文，背面戳印"官"
字铭款。春州即今广东阳春市，是南汉时期铅矿开采、
冶炼和铸造"乾亨重宝"铅钱的地方之一。

许建林先生捐赠。

Lead Ingot

The Period of Nanhan state (917-971 AD)

Length: 24.5 cm / Width: 10.0 cm / Thickness: 4.1 cm /
Weight: 6.3 kg

The front side of the lead ingot was inscribed with characters
"Chun Zhou Qian Shi Jin" (10 *Jin* lead ingot cast in Chunzhou)
and the reverse side was inscribed with the character of *"Guan"*
(officially cast). Chunzhou, modern day Yangchun of Guangdong
Province, was one of the places that lead was mined, smelted
and cast into *Qian Heng Zhong Bao* (currency of the Qianheng
Period).

It was donated by Mr.Xu Jianlin.

"乾亨重宝"铅钱

南汉国时期（公元 917 ～ 971 年）

径 2.5 ～ 2.7 厘米，重 2.5 ～ 5.0 克

始铸于南汉乾亨二年（918 年）。

2009 年南越国官署遗址出土。

Lead Coins of *"Qian Heng Zhong Bao"*

The Period of Nanhan state (917-971 AD)

Diameter: 2.5-2.7 cm/ Weight: 2.5-5.0 g

The currency was first cast in the 2nd year of Qianheng period of the Nanhan state (918 AD).

It was unearthed at the Palace Site of Nanyue state in 2009.

宋元时期，海上丝绸之路进入鼎盛。随着全国经济重心南移，航海技术的突飞猛进，广州通往世界各地的更多航线被开辟出来。

明清朝廷基本上实行"时开时禁，以禁为主"的海外贸易政策，但广州一直是开放的通商口岸，是全国与西洋进出口贸易的第一大港。明清时期，南越国宫署遗址一带仍是广州的中心—广东承宣布政使司署的所在地，直接管理着海外贸易的相关事务。清乾隆二十二年（1757年），将西洋"番商"限制在广州口岸进行贸易，使得广州的对外贸易处于垄断地位，促进了广州经济社会的发展。此后，海上丝路的管理机构由宫署遗址所在地逐渐转移至粤海关。

In Song and Yuan Dynasties, the Maritime Silk Road reached its heyday. With the national economic center moving toward south, the navigation technology developed quickly with more new sea routes established to connect Guangzhou with other parts of the world.

In the Ming and Qing Dynasties, though the court imposed the policy of ban on maritime trade at most of the time and was only open to foreign trade occasionally, Guangzhou was still an open port for foreign trade and remained the largest port for imports and exports between China and the Western countries. During the Ming and Qing Dynasties, the Palace Site of Nanyue state continued to be the center of Guangzhou as it was the location of *Guangdong Cheng Xuan Bu Zheng Shi Si* (Provincial Administration Office) which served as foreign trade intendancy. In the 22nd year of Qianlong Period of the Qing Dynasty (1757 AD), single-port-commerce system was imposed to restrict all trade with western merchants in Guangzhou port, making Guangzhou a monopoly of foreign trade in the country and boosting the economic and social development of the city. The administrational organization for the Maritime Silk Road was then gradually replaced by Guangdong Customs.

北宋开宝四年（971年），潘美率军平定南汉，广州成为广南东路经略安抚使和南海郡清海军节度使府治地，并在广州首设市舶司，由潘美兼任市舶使，管理海外贸易。在南汉国宫殿遗址之上发掘出的北宋时期的大型官署建筑基址，应为经略安抚使司署遗迹。

In the 4th year of Kaibao Period of the Northern Song Dynasty (971 AD), Pan Mei led the expeditionary force to conquer the Nanhan state. Guangzhou was made the capital of the jurisdiction of *Jing Lve An Fu Shi* (Administrative Commander) of *Guang Nan Dong Lu* (literally: Vast Southeast Guangzhou Province) and *Qinghaijun Jie Du Shi* (Regional Commander of Qinghai Military Region, roughly modern day Guangdong, Guangxi Provinces and northern Vietnam) of Nanhai Prefecture. The first *Shi Bo Si* (Maritime Trade Bureaus) was then set up in Guangzhou, where Pan Mei held the concurrent post as the first *Shi Bo Shi* (Maritime Trade Supervisor)supervising overseas trade. Large bases of government office buildings of the Northern Song Dynasty were excavated on top of the Palace Site of Nanhan state , which were speculated to be the office buildings of *Jing Lve An Fu Shi*.

潘美画像
Portrait of Pan Mei

潘美（925~991年），字仲询，大名（河北邯郸）人，北宋开国名将。开宝三年（970年），奉宋太祖赵匡胤的命令征讨岭南，开宝四年（971年）平定南汉国，随即被任命为广州知府，兼市舶使。潘美是宋代广州第一任市舶使，南海神庙的《大宋新修南海广利王庙之碑》记述了此事。

Pan Mei (925-991 AD), courtesy name Zhongxun, was born in Daming (modern day Handan, Hebei Province) and was a military general in early Northern Song Dynasty. In the 3rd year of Kaibao Period (970 AD), he led the expeditionary force to conquer Lingnan region under the order of Zhao Kuangyin, the Emperor Taizu of the Song Dynasty. In the 4th year of Kaibao Period (971 AD), he conquered the Nanhan state and was made Zhi Fu (prefect) of Guangzhou and Concurrent Shi Bo Shi (Maritime Trade Supervisor). Pan Mei was the first Shi Bo Shi of Guangzhou in the Song Dynasty and the fact was recorded in the Stele Inscription for the newly restored Temple of Dragon King of South Sea.

宋代建筑基址
The Site Base of a Building of the Song Dynasty

宋代砖铺广场
Brick-paved Square of the Song Dynasty

宋代官署庭院与水井
Courtyard and wells in the Government Office Site of the Song Dynasty

宋代庭院水池遗迹
Courtyard Pond Ruins of the Song Dynasty

青釉熏炉器盖

北宋（公元 960 ～ 1127 年）

盖径 15.3、高 10.6 厘米

熏炉主要用来熏香，所用香料大多来自海外。
2004 年南越国宫署遗址出土。

Celadon-glazed Incense Burner Cap

The Northern Song Dynasty (960-1127 AD)
Lid Diameter: 15.3cm / Height: 10.6cm

The incense burner is mainly used for scenting, and most of
the spices used are from overseas.
It was unearthed at the Palace Site of Nanyue state in 2004.

宋代对海外贸易十分重视，在广州、泉州、明州（今宁波）、杭州等地设市舶司管理海外贸易。海上丝绸之路的贸易品种由唐代的珍宝犀牙为主渐变为以进口香料和出口陶瓷贸易为主，"陶瓷之路"和"香料之路"由此闻名世界。北宋神宗熙宁十年（1077 年），明州、杭州、广州市舶司收到乳香共计三十五万多斤，仅广州一地所收乳香即多达三十四万斤，其地位远超其他港口。

The imperial court attached great importance to the foreign trade in the Song Dynasty. *Shi Bo Si* (Maritime Trade Bureaus) were set up in Guangzhou, Quanzhou, Mingzhou (modern day Ningbo) and Hangzhou. Luxury goods including rhino horns took the major part in the trade along the Maritime Silk Road in the Tang Dynasty, while in the Song Dynasty, imported incense and exported ceramics formed the major part of overseas trade. Therefore the Maritime Silk Road is also known as the Ceramics Route and the Spice Route to the world. In the 10th year of Xining Period of Emperor Shenzong of the Northern Song Dynasty (1077 AD), *shi Bo si* of Mingzhou, Hangzhou and Guangzhou received a total of 350,000 *jin* of imported frankincense, of which 340,000 *jin* was imported via Guangzhou. This showed the predominant position of Guangzhou among the ports of foreign trade then.

陶熏炉

明代（公元 1368 ~ 1644 年）
残高 30.7、炉口径 15.6 厘米

用来熏香的香炉，底座和炉盆套接而成。
2004 年南越国宫署遗址出土。

Ceramic Incense Burner

The Ming Dynasty (1368-1644 AD)
Residual Height: 30.7cm / Mouth Diameter: 15.6 cm

The incense burner used for scenting is formed by a base and a burner basin.
It was unearthed at the Palace Site of Nanyue state in 2004.

宋代广州香料贸易
Incense Trade in Guangzhou in the Song Dynasty

名称 Name	产地 Origin	用途 Usage
乳香 Frankincense	主产于阿拉伯半岛东南部和非洲索马里 Native to the Southeast of the Arabian Peninsula and Somalia of Arfica	药用、熏香 Medicine, burning incense
檀香 Sandalwood	分布于印度、马来西亚、澳大利亚及印度尼西亚等地。中国台湾亦有栽培 Distributed in India, Malaysia, Australia and Indonesia. It is also cultivated in Taiwan, China	药用、祀佛、建筑 Medicine, religious offering, building material
麝香 Musk	主产于中国四川、西藏、云南、陕西、甘肃、内蒙古等地 Native to Sichuan, Tibet, Yunnan, Shaanxi, Gansu and Inner Mongolia Provinces of China	熏香、药用 Burning incense, medicine
沉香 Agarwood	分布于越南和中国广东、海南、广西、福建等地 Distributed in Vietnam and Guangdong, Hainan, Guangxi and Fujian Provinces of China	熏香、药用、祭祀敬神、建筑 Burning incense, medicine, religious offering, building material
龙涎香 Ambergris	分布于太平洋、南太平洋群岛附近 Distributed in Pacific and South Pacific Islands	熏香、药用 Burning incense, medicine
丁香 Clove	分布于印度尼西亚、印度、越南、巴基斯坦、斯里兰卡等地 Distributed in Indonesia, India, Vietnam, Pakistan, Sri Lanka, etc	药用、涂香 Medicine, paste incense
木香 Costus Root	分布于中国陕西、甘肃、湖北、湖南、云南等地 Distributed in Shaanxi, Gansu, Hubei, Hunan and Yuannan Provinces of China	熏烧、涂香、药用 Burning incense, paste incense, medicine
龙脑香 Borneolum	主产于印度尼西亚婆罗洲北部、苏门答腊岛及马来西亚等地区 Native to northern Borneo of Indonesia, Sumatera Island and Malaysia, etc.	熏烧、涂香、祀佛、药用 Burning incense, paste incense, religious offering, medicine
降真香 Rosewood	分布于马来西亚、印度尼西亚婆罗洲北部、苏门答腊岛、泰国、越南、柬埔寨和中国广东、广西、云南等地 Distributed in Malaysia, northern Borneo of Indonesia, Sumatera Island, Thailand, Vietnam, Cambodia and Guangdong, Guangxi and Yunnan Provinces of China	熏烧、药用、染色 Burning incense, medicine, dyeing

隋唐时期，广州已发展成为东方第一大港，宋代以来陶瓷也日渐成为中国对外贸易的大宗商品，在此背景下，广东陶瓷制造业迅速发展。近年来，在配合广州城市建设过程进行的考古发掘中，特别是在被誉为岭南两千年中心地的南越国宫署遗址，出土有西村窑、佛山窑、笔架山窑、湖田窑、闽清义窑、同安窑、龙泉窑等地窑口的陶瓷器。结合文献记载，宋元时期，广东和全国各地名窑产品大多汇集广州，经由广州港中转出口至海外各国，这对推动广州城市和社会发展起到重要作用。

Under the background that Guangzhou had developed into the biggest port of the East World in Sui and Tang Dynasties while ceramics gradually became the major commodities in overseas trade from the Song Dynasty, ceramic manufacturing of Guangzhou boomed in that period. In recent archaeological excavations cooperating with city construction of Guangzhou, especially in the Palace Site of Nanyue State which was the center of the two-thousand-year civilization of Lingnan, ceramics of Xicun, Foshan, Bijiashan, Hutian, Tong'an, Longquan Kilns as well as Yi Kiln of Minqing County have been unearthed. According to documentary records, in Song and Yuan Dynasties, most of the products from famous kilns nationwide gathered in Guangzhou and exported overseas via Guangzhou Port, which greatly promoted the urban and social development of Guangzhou.

西村窑

西村窑是北宋时期以烧制青瓷和青白瓷为主的民间窑场，窑址位于广州市西村增涉河东岸岗地上。日常生活用器类品种繁多，兼有杂器玩具，装饰手法有刻花、划花、印花、彩绘和镂孔等。西村窑的产品远销海内外，近年来在我国西沙群岛和东南亚、南亚、西亚等地区多有出水或出土。

Xicun Kiln

It was a large-sized nongovernmental kiln in Guangzhou in the Northern Song Dynasty, which mainly produced celadon and greenish white porcelain wares. The kiln site is on the hillock of the east bank of Zengshe River in Xicun Village, Guangzhou. The kiln produced a great variety of daily utensils as well as some miscellaneous articles and toys. Decorative techniques such as relief, impressing, color painting, stippling and hollowing-out were used. Xicun Kiln wares were widely sold both in and out of its home country, some of which were discovered in Xisha Islands of China as well as Southeast Asia, South Asia and West Asia in recent years.

西村窑址出土的陶瓷标本
Ceramic Samples Unearthed in Xicun Kiln Site

2015 年印度尼西亚海域打捞出水的西村窑青瓷彩绘花卉纹大盘
Celadon Plates with Floral Pattern of Xicun Kiln Found in Indonesian Waters in 2015

西村窑青釉缠枝牡丹纹盆

北宋（公元 960 ~ 1127 年）

口径 33.6、高 9.2 厘米

敞口，口沿外撇，弧腹，矮圈足。器内上腹部刻划一周缠枝牡丹纹，近底部饰一周旋纹。
浅灰胎，胎质粗松，釉呈青灰色，足底露胎。器体比较大。
1997 年南越国宫署遗址出土。

Celadon Basin with the Pattern of Peony and Tangled Branches, Xicun Kiln

The Northern Song Dynasty (960-1127 AD)
Mouth Diameter: 33.6cm / Height: 9.2cm

It has an open mouth with the edge folding outwards, arc abdomen and a short ring foot. The inside of
the upper abdomen is carved with a circle of the pattern of peony and tangled branches, while the bottom
is decorated with a circle of revolved lines. The body is rough and slack , the color of which is light gray.
The glaze appears bluish gray and the body is exposed at the bottom of the foot. It is quite big.
It was unearthed at the Palace Site of Nanyue state in 1997.

西村窑青釉军持

北宋（公元 960 ～ 1127 年）
口径 9.8、高 28.2 厘米

口微敛，口沿外展成凸棱，长颈，圆鼓腹，矮圈足，肩上有一斜向上锥形流嘴，肩部和腹部各饰一道旋纹。军持是佛教徒和伊斯兰教徒的净手器。
1997 年南越国宫苑遗址出土。

Celadon Kendi, Xicun Kiln

The Northern Song Dynasty (960-1127 AD)
Mouth Diameter: 9.8cm / Height: 28.2cm

The mouth slightly shrinks inwardly, and the edge extends outside to form the protruding edge. It has a long neck, round and plump abdomen and a short ring foot, with an up-inclined and cone-shaped spout at the shoulder. Revolved lines are used to decorate the shoulder and the abdomen respectively. Kendi is a hand washing tool for Buddhists and Islamites.

It was unearthed at the site of the royal garden of Nanyue state in 1997.

西村窑青釉褐彩绘花卉纹军持

北宋（公元 960 ~ 1127 年）

口径 8.3、高 17.5 厘米

口沿、流嘴和下腹部施青黄釉，颈、肩和腹部绘三道褐彩弦纹，上腹部绘
褐彩缠枝花卉纹。

2003 年南越国宫署遗址出土。

Celadon Kendi with Brown-Colored Floral Pattern, Xicun Kiln

The Northern Song Dynasty (960-1127 AD)
Mouth Diameter: 8.3cm / Height: 17.5cm

The mouth edge, spout and lower abdomen are decorated with greenish yellow glaze.
The neck, shoulder and abdomen of the kendi are decorated with three strokes of
brown bow-string patterns, while the upper abdomen is painted with the pattern of
brown flower and tangled branches.
It was unearthed at the Palace Site of Nanyue state in 2003.

西村窑青釉执壶

北宋（公元 960 ~ 1127 年）
口径 9.1、高 17.4 厘米

撇口，长颈，瓜棱形腹，圈足，肩上一侧安弧形流嘴，另一侧有双股藤状执把。
足底露胎，浅灰色胎，胎质较粗松，釉色青灰泛黄。
2005 年南越国宫署遗址出土。

Celadon Ewer, Xicun Kiln

The Northern Song Dynasty (960-1127 AD)
Mouth Diameter: 9.1cm / Height: 17.4cm

It has an evaginated mouth, a long neck, melon prismatic abdomen and a ring foot, with a curved spout on one side of its shoulder and a double-stranded and rattan-like holder on the other side. The body is exposed at the bottom of the foot. The body is rough and slack with light gray color, and the glaze is in yellowish grey color.
It was unearthed at the Palace Site of Nanyue state in 2005.

笔架山窑

　　窑址位于潮州市区韩江东岸的笔架山，始烧于唐末五代，宋代在景德镇等地瓷窑烧造技术和工艺的基础上创新发展，生产出大量的优质瓷器并远销海外。以烧制青白瓷、青瓷为主，也有黑釉、白釉瓷等，胎多呈白色或灰白色，胎质细腻坚致。器类包括碗、盘、碟、瓶、炉、罐、执壶等，还有人物和动物瓷塑，种类繁多。器物纹饰以划花为主，其次是雕刻、贴花、镂空等。

Bijiashan Kiln

　　The kiln site is located on Bijiashan Mountain, on the east bank of Hanjiang River in Chaozhou City. Initiated in the late Tang Dynasty and the Five Dynasties, the kiln innovated and further developed the porcelain kiln firing technology of Jingdezhen kiln and other kilns in the Song Dynasty, producing a large amount of high-quality porcelain for overseas markets. It produced mainly the greenish white porcelain and celadon, as well as some black or white-glazed porcelain, etc. Most of the porcelain bodies are white or grayish white, and the bodies are delicate and firm. The porcelain types include bowls, plates, dishes, bottles, stoves, pots, ewers, as well as figurines and animal figurines, etc. The porcelain is mainly decorated with incised flowers, and then carved patterns, decals, hollowed-out patterns and so on.

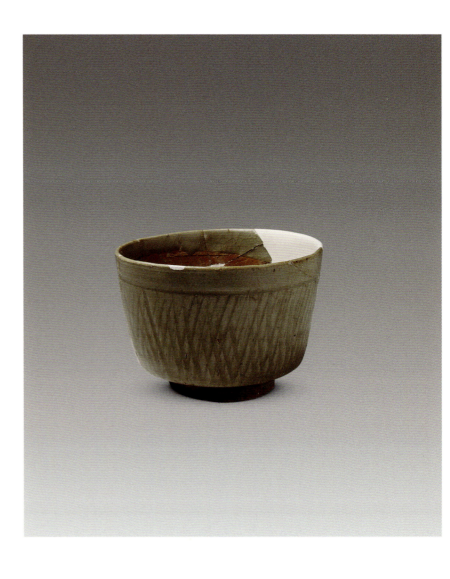

笔架山窑青白瓷网格纹炉

宋代（公元 960 ~ 1279 年）
口径 12.1、高 8.5 厘米

直口，深直腹，圈足。器口和外腹部施青白釉。外口沿下饰一周旋纹，外腹部刻饰网格纹。
2004 年南越国宫署遗址出土。

Greenish White Porcelain Furnace with Grid Patter, Bijiashan Kiln

The Song Dynasty (960-1279 AD)
Mouth Diameter: 12.1cm / Height: 8.5cm

It has a straight mouth, deep straight abdomen and a ring foot. The mouth and outer abdomen are greenish-white-glazed, with a circle of revolved lines at the outer mouth edge and grid pattern carved on the outer abdomen.
It was unearthed at the Palace Site of Nanyue state in 2004.

笔架山窑青白瓷划花纹碟

宋代（公元 960 ~ 1279 年）

口径 13.8、高 4.4 厘米

撇口，浅弧腹，圈足较高，器足内无釉。器内口沿饰一周旋纹，内底划一折枝牡丹纹。

1995 年南越国宫署遗址出土。

Greenish White Porcelain Dish with Incised Floral Patterns, Bijiashan Kiln

The Song Dynasty (960-1279 AD)

Mouth Diameter: 13.8cm / Height: 4.4cm

It has an evaginated mouth, shallow arc abdomen, a high ring foot and there is no glaze inside the foot. A circle of revolved lines is decorated at the mouth edge while the pattern of peony twig is decorated at the inner bottom.

It was unearthed at the Palace Site of Nanyue state in 1995.

佛山窑

　　佛山窑是我国陶瓷史上著名的民窑，形成于唐宋时期，繁盛于明清时期，流传发展至今。宋代的窑场主要分布在今广东省佛山市石湾镇的大帽岗、小塘镇的奇石村和官窑镇的文头岭，三地的器物无论在胎质、釉色、烧造方法上都基本一致。以烧制罐、盆、碗、碟、炉等日用陶瓷为主，胎质较粗，多呈灰色或灰白色，釉以青黄色或酱褐色居多。佛山境内有优质的瓷土，且水网发达，交通方便，毗邻广州，佛山窑的产品通过广州远销至日本和东南亚等地。

Foshan Kiln

Foshan Kiln is a famous nongovern-mental kiln in the history of China's ceramics. It was formed in Tang and Song Dynasties, then flourished in Ming and Qing Dynasties and has been developing till today. The kilns in the Song Dynasty were mainly distributed in Damao Hillock of Shiwan Town, Qishi Village of Xiaotang Town, and Wentou Ridge of Guanyao Town, Foshan City, Guangdong Province, and the artifacts produced in the three places were basically the same in terms of body, glaze color and firing methods. The kilns mainly fired pots, basins, bowls, dishes, stoves and other daily-use ceramics. The products featured rough bodies which was mostly gray or grayish white, and the glaze was mostly greenish yellow or brown. Foshan stays next to Guangzhou, and owns high-quality porcelain clay, densely distributed canal and river networks and convenient transportation. The products from Foshan Kiln were exported to Japan, Southeast Asia and other places via Guangzhou.

佛山窑酱黄釉炉

宋代（公元 960 ～ 1279 年）
口径 10.7、高 7 厘米

侈口，平折沿，深直腹，足座较矮，底沿折起。器口和炉体外腹部施酱黄色釉。2004 年南越国宫署遗址出土。

Brownish-Yellow-Glazed Furnace, Foshan Kiln

The Song Dynasty (960-1279 AD)
Mouth Diameter: 10.7cm / Height: 7cm

It has a wide-flared mouth with flat-folded edge, deep straight abdomen and a short foot seat which is folded at the bottom edge. The mouth and the outer abdomen of the furnace are brownish-yellow-glazed.
It was unearthed at the Palace Site of Nanyue state in 2004.

佛山窑青釉龙纹四耳罐

宋代（公元 960 ～ 1279 年）

口径 9.6、高 27 厘米

侈口，卷圆唇，束颈，圆鼓腹，平底。颈肩处安四个横条形耳，肩部贴塑一龙纹。器口至近腹底部施青黄色釉。

2006 年南越国宫署遗址出土。

Celadon Pot, Foshan Kiln

The Song Dynasty (960-1279 AD)
Mouth Diameter: 9.6cm / Height: 27cm

It has a wide-flared mouth, a curved and round lip, a bundled neck, round and inflated abdomen and a flat bottom. At the neck and shoulder there are four strip-typed ears with a dragon pattern laminated. Greenish yellow glaze is applied from the mouth to the place near the bottom of its abdomen.

It was unearthed at the Palace Site of Nanyue state in 2006.

湖田窑

　　湖田窑是五代至明代著名的窑场，窑址位于江西省景德镇市区东南的湖田村。五代以烧制青瓷器为主，宋代以生产青白瓷而名闻天下，元代生产卵白釉瓷和青花瓷器等。器形以碗、盘、碟、盏、炉、执壶、枕等日常生活器具为主，装饰有刻花、划花、印花、篦划等技法，产品远销海内外。

Hutian Kiln

　　It was a famous kiln from the Five Dynasties to the Ming Dynasty. The kiln site is located in Hutian Village, the southeast of Jingdezhen City, Jiangxi Province. It fired mainly celadon porcelain in the Five Dynasties, became known for producing greenish white porcelain in the Song Dynasty, and manufactured egg-white glazed porcelain as well as blue and white porcelain in the Yuan Dynasty. The porcelain wares were mainly bowls, plates, dishes, small cups, furnaces, ewers, pillows and other daily utensils, which were decorated with carved, incised, impressed, combed patterns, and sold to local and overseas markets.

湖田窑青白瓷刻花卉纹盘

宋代（公元 960 ~ 1279 年）

口径 19.6、高 5.4 厘米

六出花口，敞口，上腹斜直，下腹折收，内底近平，圈足，足底较厚。器内腹底部刻花卉纹。1997 年南越国宫苑遗址出土。

Greenish white Porcelain Plate with Carved Floral Pattern, Hutian Kiln

The Song Dynasty (960-1279 AD)

Mouth Diameter: 19.6cm / Height: 5.4cm

It has an open mouth with six petal-like angles. Its upper abdomen is oblique but straight, while its lower abdomen is folded inwards. It has a nearly flat inner bottom and a ring foot with thick bottom. Inside the ware there are carved floral patterns.
It was unearthed at the site of the royal garden of Nanyue state in 1997.

湖田窑青白瓷狮形枕

宋代（公元 960 ～ 1279 年）

长 17.5、残高 9.8 厘米

由枕面、狮形座和底板三部分黏结而成，底板已残缺。狮背顶如意状枕面，狮子张嘴露齿，怒目圆睁，背篦划鬃毛。

2009 年南越国宫署遗址出土。

Greenish white Porcelain Lion-shaped Pillow, Hutian Kiln

The Song Dynasty (960-1279 AD)

Length: 17.5cm / Residual Height: 9.8cm

The pillow is made up of three parts: pillow surface, lion-shaped base and bottom plate. The bottom plate is partially missing. The pillow surface is like a *ruyi* (an S-shaped ornamental object) on the back of the lion. The lion opens lits mouth and shows its teeth, with its eyes staring angrily. On its back the hairs are combed out.

It was unearthed at the Palace Site of Nanyue state in 2009.

湖田窑青白瓷盏

宋代（公元 960 ~ 1279 年）

口径 11.6、高 4.2 厘米

荷叶状花口，斜弧腹，圈足。足底露胎，釉色青白泛黄。器内由口至底划
出叶脉状纹，内底心模印花瓣纹。

2003 年南越国宫署遗址出土。

Greenish white Porcelain Small Cup, Hutian Kiln

The Song Dynasty (960-1279 AD)
Mouth Diameter: 11.6cm / Height: 4.2cm

The small cup has a lotus-leaf-like mouth, oblique arc abdomen,and a ring foot with
base exposed at the bottom. The glaze is in yellowish greenish white color. Inside the
cup, leaf vein patterns are incised from the mouth to the bottom, with the petal pattern
impressed on the inner bottom.

It was unearthed at the Palace Site of Nanyue state in 2003.

同安窑

　　同安窑位于福建同安汀溪、新民和翔安内厝一带，是一处以生产青瓷而著名的宋元时期大型民间窑场。其产品釉青泛黄，尤以枇杷黄最佳，因其刻划花卉、篦线、篦点纹等流畅自然，深受日本"茶汤鼻祖"村田珠光高僧喜爱，因而又被称为"珠光青瓷"。

Tong'an Kiln

　　Tong'an Kiln is located near Tingxi Town and Xinmin Town of Tong'an District, and Neicuo Town of Xiang'an District, Xiamen, Fujian Province. In Song and Yuan Dynasties, it was a big nongovernmental kiln known for producing celadon. The products featured the yellowish green glaze, especially the loquat yellow. With smooth and natural carved and incised patterns of flowers, combed lines and dots, they were much favored by the Japanese eminent monk Murata Jukō, the founder of the Japanese tea ceremony, and hence known as Jukō Celadon.

同安窑青瓷篦划纹碗

宋代（公元 960 ～ 1279 年）
口径 16、高 6.2 厘米

束口，口沿外侈，斜直腹，矮圈足，内底凹窝状。器内满釉，器外施釉不到底，釉青泛黄。内腹饰篦划纹，外壁划复线纹。
2003 年南越国宫署遗址出土。

Celadon Bowl with Combed Pattern, Tong'an Kiln

The Song Dynasty (960-1279 AD)
Mouth Diameter: 16cm / Height: 6.2cm

It has a bundled mouth, oblique but straight abdomen and a short ring foot. Its mouth edge folds outwards and its inner bottom dents inwards. The inside surface of the ware is fully glazed, while the outer surface is glazed except for the bottom. The glaze appears yellowish green. The inner abdomen is decorated with combed pattern, and the outer abdomen is with complex line pattern.
It was unearthed at the Palace Site of Nanyue state in 2003.

龙泉窑

　　龙泉窑位于浙江境内，其烧造时间从宋至清，瓷釉厚润，釉色青翠。其产品畅销于亚洲、非洲、欧洲的许多国家和地区，影响十分深远。

Longquan Kiln

Longquan Kiln is located in Zhejiang Province. It fired porcelain from the Song Dynasty to the Qing Dynasty. The glaze of its porcelain is thick and smooth with verdant color. Its products sold well in many countries and regions in Asia, Africa and Europe and had a far-reaching influence.

龙泉窑青瓷花口盘

元代（公元 1206 ~ 1368 年）
口径 33.2、高 6 厘米

菱花口，平折沿，浅弧腹，圈足。
2003 年南越国宫署遗址出土。

Celadon Plate with Petal-like Mouth, Longquan Kiln

The Yuan Dynasty (1206-1368 AD)
Mouth Diameter: 33.2cm / Height: 6cm

The plate has a petal-like mouth with flatly folded edge, shallow arc abdomen and a ring foot.
It was unearthed at the Palace Site of Nanyue state in 2003.

义窑

义窑位于福建省闽清县东桥镇义由村、青由村一带，以生产青白瓷、青瓷为主，系宋元时期重要的外销瓷窑厂。器形以碗、盘、碟、壶、罐等日常生活器为主，纹饰以刻划莲花、菊瓣纹居多。

Yi Kiln

Yi Kiln is located near Yiyou Village and Qingyou Village in Dongqiao Town, Minqing County, Fujian Province. It mainly produced greenish white porcelain and celadon wares and is known as one of the major porcelain export kilns in Song and Yuan Dynasties. The porcelain products were mainly bowls, plates, dishes, kettles, pots and other daily utensils, which were mostly decorated with carved patterns of lotus and daisy petals.

义窑青白瓷刻折枝莲纹碟

元代（公元 1206 ～ 1368 年）
口径 15 厘米

敞口，折腹，平底微内凹。灰白胎，青白釉，釉色泛青，外底露胎。内底刻划一折枝莲纹，娇艳欲滴，惹人喜爱。
2004 年南越国宫署遗址出土。

Greenish white Porcelain Dish with Carved Pattern of Lotus Twig, Yi Kiln

The Yuan Dynasty (1206-1368 AD)
Mouth Diameter: 15cm

The dish has an open mouth, folded abdomen and a flat bottom which caves in slightly. It features the greyish white body and greenish white glaze which appears a little greenish. The body is exposed on the outer bottom. Inside the bottom there is a carved lotus twig, which is delicate, charming and endearing.
It was unearthed at the Palace Site of Nanyue state in 2004.

明清广东布政司署建筑遗迹

　　明洪武九年（1376 年）撤销行中书省，以后陆续分为十三个承宣布政使司，是最高的省级行政机构。南越国宫署遗址内发掘出明清广东承宣布政司署遗迹和墨书"广东布政□使"文字瓦片，证明明清两代近六百年统治中，广州的政治中心位于南越国宫署遗址一带。广东布政司直接管理着海外贸易相关事务，直到 1757 年此项功能才逐渐转移至粤海关。

The Building Remains of Guangdong *Bu Zheng Si Shu* (Provincial Administration Commission Office) in Ming and Qing Dynasties

　　In the 9th year of Hongwu Period of the Ming Dynasty (1376 AD), *Xing Zhong Shu Sheng* (provincial administration system taken over from the Yuan Dynasty) were dissolved and 13 *Bu Zheng Shi Si* (Provincial Administration Commissions) were established as top provincial administrative organizations. The site of Guangdong Provincial Administration Commission Office in Ming and Qing Dynasties and the tile piece with inked Chinese characters of "*Guang Dong Bu Zheng* □ *Shi* (Provincial Administration Commission of Guangdong)" of the Ming Dynasty excavated from the Palace Site of Nanyue state are evidences that the location was the center of Guangzhou and the site of provincial government in about 600 years during Ming and Qing Dynasties. The provincial government had been directly overseeing the affairs related to overseas trade until the year of 1757 when the function was taken by Guangzhou Customs.

清代广东布政司署遗迹（航拍）
Remains of Guangdong Provincial Administration Commission
Office in the Qing Dynasty (aerial photo)

清代广东布政司署遗址局部
Remains of Guangdong Provincial Administration Commission
Office in the Qing Dynasty – Partial View

清代广东布政司署门楼与过道
Remains of Guangdong Provincial Administration Commission
Office in the Qing Dynasty–Gatehouse and Corridor

墨书"广东布政□使"文字瓦片

明代（公元 1368 ～ 1644 年）

长 13.8、宽 9.6 厘米

2004 年南越国宫署遗址出土。

Tile Piece with Inked Chinese Characters of "*Guang Dong Bu Zheng* □ *Shi*"

The Ming Dynasty (1368-1644 AD)

Length: 13.8cm / Width: 9.6 cm

It was unearthed at the Palace Site of Nanyue state in 2004.

漳州窑青花双鹿花卉纹盘

明代（公元 1368 ~ 1644 年）

直径 22、高 4 厘米

克拉克瓷，这是欧洲人对明末清初来自中国、具体产地不明的青花瓷器的统称。后经考古发掘得知，这些瓷器多产于福建漳州地区，以连续开光图案装饰为特点，纹饰繁缛，深受欧洲王公贵族喜爱。

2003 年南越国宫署遗址出土。

Blue and White Porcelain Plate with the Pattern of Double Deer and Flowers, Zhangzhou Kiln

The Ming Dynasty (1368-1644 AD)

Diameter: 22cm / Height: 4 cm

Clark porcelain is the European collective name for the blue and white porcelains from China with unknown origin in late Ming and early Qing Dynasties. After archaeological excavations, it was learned that such porcelain wares were mostly produced in Zhangzhou area of Fujian Province characterized by continuous blessing pattern and elaborate ornamentation, and they were much favored by European nobles.

It was unearthed at the Palace Site of Nanyue state in 2003.

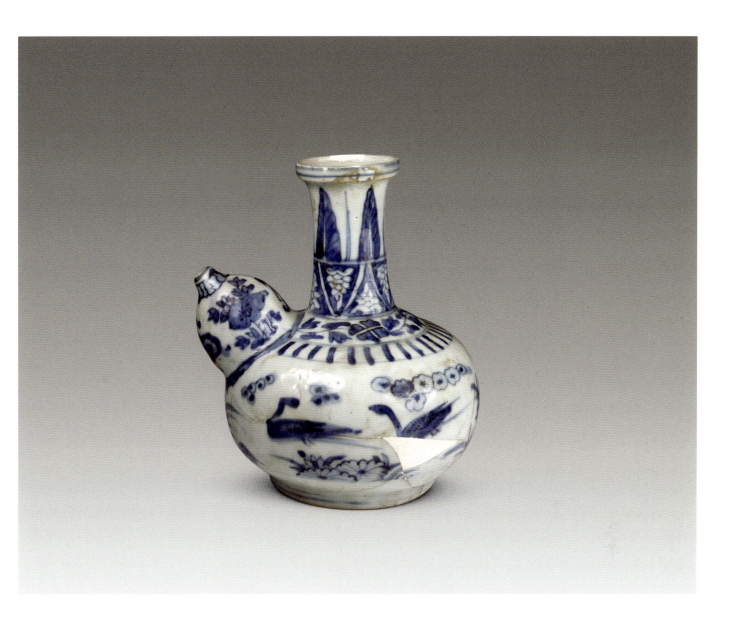

景德镇窑青花雁鸭花卉纹军持

明代（公元 1368 ~ 1644 年）

口径 5.5、高 18.4 厘米

2003 年南越国宫署遗址出土。

Blue and White Porcelain Kendi with the Pattern of Wild Geese. Ducks and Flowers, Jingdezhen Kiln

The Ming Dynasty (1368-1644 AD)
Mouth Diameter: 5.5cm / Height: 18.4 cm

It was unearthed at the Palace Site of Nanyue state in 2003.

景德镇窑青花加彩石榴梅菊纹盘

清代（公元 1644 ~ 1911 年）

口径 21.9 厘米

青花加彩以其高贵艳丽的特色，深受海外诸国喜爱，图案也常为外销而精心设计。

2003 年南越国宫署遗址出土。

Blue and White Porcelain Plate with Pomegranate, Plum Blossom and Chrysanthemum Pattern, Jingdezhen Kiln

The Qing Dynasty (1644-1911 AD)

Mouth Diameter: 21.9cm

Characterized by their noble and gorgeous appearance, blue and white porcelains with powder enamel were much welcome in overseas markets, and their patterns were usually elaborately designed for export.

It was unearthed at the Palace Site of Nanyue state in 2003.

景德镇窑青花山水人物盘

清代（公元 1644 ~ 1911 年）

长 31.8、宽 24.7、高 3.6 厘米

中国人物故事、山水建筑、动物花卉等是外销瓷器常用图案。瓷器绘画是西方人了解中国的重要途径。
2003 年南越国宫署遗址出土。

Blue and White Porcelain Plate with the Pattern of Landscape and Chinese Figures, Jingdezhen Kiln

The Qing Dynasty (1644-1911 AD)
Length: 31.8cm / Width: 24.7cm / Height: 3.6cm

Stories of Chinese figures, landscapes and architectures, animals and flowers and so on are common patterns found on the porcelains exported to other countries. Porcelain painting is an important way for westerners to understand China.
It was unearthed at the Palace Site of Nanyue state in 2003.

四

遗址保护 海丝申遗

The Preservation of Cultural Heritage

以"文物保护为主"的理念始终贯穿于南越国宫署遗址的考古发掘工作中，南越国宫署遗址作为国家"十一五"期间 100 处大遗址保护项目中广东的唯一入选项目，肩负着重要的保护责任。南越国—南汉国宫署遗址是广州海上丝绸之路重要史迹点之一，见证了广州两千余年海外商贸与文化交流持续发展与繁荣的历程。2016 年，南越国—南汉国宫署遗址被国家文物局列入"海上丝绸之路首批申遗遗产点"，南越王宫博物馆的海丝保护和申遗工作进入新阶段。

The concept of "cultural heritage conservation first" has been implemented throughout the archaeological excavations of the Palace Site of Nanyue state. The Site was enlisted in the "100 National Conservation Key Great Sites" project during the 11th Five-Year Plan which is the only one from Guangdong Province. The Palace site of Nanyue and Nanhan states is one of the most important historical sites of the Maritime Silk Road in Guangzhou, as it has been witnessing the continuing development and lasting prosperity of foreign trade and cultural exchange in Guangzhou for more than 2,000 years. In 2016, it was enlisted by the State Bureau of Cultural Relics as one of the first sites of the Maritime Silk Road for the UNESCO World Cultural Heritage application. This marked a new stage for the Archaeological Site Museum of Nanyue Palace in preservation of the cultural heritage of the Maritime Silk Road and preparation for the World Cultural Heritage application.

考古发掘

The Archaeological Excavation

　　南越国宫署遗址的发现和发掘工作大致可分为三个阶段：第一阶段为1975～1998年，为配合城市建设进行的抢救性发掘，其中1995年、1997年发现南越国宫苑的石水池和曲流石渠遗迹，这两次发掘均被评为当年"全国十大考古新发现"；第二阶段是2000年在儿童公园内的试掘，发现南越国宫殿遗迹，确认南越国宫殿区的位置；第三阶段为2002～2009年，根据试掘结果，在原儿童公园内进行大规模的主动发掘，先后发掘出西汉南越国和五代十国南汉国的宫殿遗迹，以及秦汉至民国时期的文化遗存。发掘表明，南越国宫署遗址是广州两千年来作为岭南地区政治、经济、文化中心地以及广州海上丝绸之路发展和持续繁荣的重要历史见证。

The discovery and excavation work of the Palace site of Nanyue state can be divided into three stages. The 1st stage was from 1975-1998, in the rescue archaeological excavations along with the city's urban infrastructure construction, in the year of 1995 and 1997, a stone pond and a meandering canal in the royal garden of Nanyue state were discovered and both these two excavations were enlisted in the top ten national archaeological discoveries of the year. The 2nd stage was the trial excavation in the Children's Park in 2000, with remains of Nanyue palace found and the location of the palace identified. The 3rd stage was from 2002 to 2009, a large-scale excavation was carried out in the former Children's Park and the Palace Site of Nanyue and Nanhan states along with other cultural relics from the Qin and Han Dynasties to the Republic of China unearthed. The Palace Site of Nanyue state has witnessed over 2,000 years of history of Guangzhou being the political, economic, and cultural center of Lingnan region, as well as the development and continuous prosperity of Guangzhou Maritime Silk Road.

1975年秦代造船遗迹发掘现场
The Excavation Scene of Remains of Shipbuilding in the Qin Dynasty in 1975

1997年南越国宫苑曲流石渠发掘现场
The Excavation Scene of the Meandering Canal of the Royal Garden of Nanyue state in 1997

2003 年南越国砖石走道发掘现场
The Excavation Scene of the Brick-and-Stone-Paved Aisleway of Nanyue state in 2003

2000 年考古人员在清理南越国一号宫殿基址
The Archaeologists Cleaning Up the Base of No. 1 Palace of
Nanyue state in 2000

考古人员在清理唐代灰坑
The Archaeologist Cleaning up a Pit of the Tang Dynasty

科学保护
The Scientific Conservation

在国家文物局和广东省有关部门的大力支持和指导下，中共广州市委、市政府对南越国一南汉国宫署遗址的保护高度重视，并作出多项决定：对遗址进行原址保护，成立专门保护管理机构，划定遗址保护范围和建设控制地带，拨专款搬迁儿童公园，由文物部门进行专项考古发掘与保护等。2008 年，广州市委、市政府决定依托遗址建立南越王宫博物馆（一期）。2011 年 1 月，成立南越王宫博物馆，负责遗址的考古发掘、遗产保护、科学研究、展示利用和日常管理等工作。2014 年 5 月 1 日，博物馆全面建成并对外开放，现已成为广州一张响亮的历史文化名片，对提升广州城市文化软实力，保护和传承岭南文化发挥了积极作用，取得了良好的社会效益。

Under the instruction and support of the State Bureau of Cultural Relics and other provincial departments, Guangzhou Municipal CPC committee and municipal government have attached great importance to the conservation of the Palace Site of Nanyue and Nanhan states and published several decrees, including in-situ conservation of the site, establishment of specialized conservation administration agency, delimiting conservation area and constructing control area, allocating special fund to relocate the Children's Park, as well as conducting special projects for archaeological excavations and conservation. In 2008, Guangzhou Municipal CPC committee and Guang zhou municipal government decided to set up the Archaeological Site Museum of Nanyue Palace (Phase I) based on the Site. In January 2011, The Archaeological Site Museum of Nanyue Palace was founded in charge of the excavation, conservation, research, exhibition as well as the daily management of the museum. On May 1, 2014, the museum was completed and opened to the public, which now has become a prominent historical cultural card of Guangzhou. The museum plays a positive role in the promotion of the cultural soft power of Guangzhou as well as the conservation and inheritance of Lingnan culture, meantime gaining good social benefits.

1998 年 1 月 9 日，国家文物局派出由张柏副局长率领的包括宿白、徐苹芳、黄景略、郑孝燮、傅熹年、罗哲文、张忠培、李伯谦、傅连兴、刘庆柱、李准、王丹华、辛占山等 13 位多学科专家组成的专家组考察南越国宫苑曲流石渠遗址发掘现场。

On January 9, 1998, a 13-member multidisciplinary expert team led by Zhang Bai, deputy director of the State Bureau of Cultural Relics, inspected the excavation scene of the meandering canal in the royal garden of Nanyue state. The experts included Su Bai, Xu Pingfang, Huang Jinglue, Zheng Xiaoxie, Fu Xinian, Luo Zhewen, Zhang Zhongpei, Li Boqian, Fu Lianxing, Liu Qingzhu, Li Zhun, Wang Danhua and Xin Zhanshan.

1998 年 1 月 10 日，国家文物局在广州市政府礼堂召开"南越国宫署遗址广州论证会"，认为南越国宫苑遗址是迄今为止发现年代最早的中国宫苑实例，对研究中国历史文化、中国古代城市（特别是古代广州城）、古代建筑史和古代工艺史有极其重要的价值，是广州历史文化名城的精华所在。

On January 10, 1998, the State Bureau of Cultural Relics held a conference on the Palace Site of Nanyue state in the auditorium of Guangzhou municipal government. It was believed that the Palace Site of Nanyue state was the earliest example among Chinese palaces discovered so far and was of great value to the study of Chinese history and culture, ancient Chinese cities (especially ancient Guangzhou City), ancient architectural history and ancient technological history. Therefore, the site represents the best part of Guangzhou as a famous historical city.

1997 年 12 月 18 日，国家文物局张文彬局长考察南越国宫苑遗址时指出，一定要保护好遗址，并希望能把儿童公园范围内的宫殿区揭露出来。这样，就有条件申报世界文化遗产。

On December 18, 1997, then director of the State Bureau of Cultural Relics, Zhang Wenbin, inspected the royal garden site of Nanyue state. He stressed that the site must be well conserved, and hoped that the palace area within the range of the Children's Park could also be disclosed so as to apply for the World Cultural Heritage.

广 州 市 人 民 政 府

关于保护南越国宫署遗址的通告

穗府〔1998〕62 号

　　南越国宫署遗址于 1995 年 7 月在本市中山四路地段被发现，并于 1996 年 11 月被国务院列为国家重点文物保护单位。为加强对该文物的保护和管理，根据国家《文物保护法》及有关规定，结合本市实际，特通告如下：
　　一、南越国宫署遗址是中国历史文化瑰宝，是广州历史文化名城的精华所在。该遗址的保护、建设和管理纳入广州市城市总体规划。
　　二、南越国宫署遗址保护控制范围暂定为：东起中山四路忠佑大街、城隍庙和长胜里以西；南至中山四路规划路北边线；西至北京路东边线；北至梯云里、儿童公园后墙和省财政厅以南地段。总面积为 4.8 万平方米。
　　三、在遗址保护区内不得进行任何危害文物遗址的建设工程。保护区内已按城市规划安排建设单位（含房地产开发单位）的建设用地，需要建设的，必须先进行地下文物勘探，确认与地下文物保护无矛盾后，按《文物保护法》规定的审批程序报经批准后方可进行。
　　四、凡在遗址保护区内急需抢救维修的危房，原则上按原状修复，不得加建或改建。维修项目必须报市文化局同意后，再按市规划局批准。
　　五、遗址保护区内原则上不迁入新户口。因出生、婚姻、继承、产权交易等需迁入的，按有关规定办理。
　　六、公安、司法、规划、国土房管、城监和文化行政管理等部门，要相互配合，密切协作，做好文物遗址的保护和管理工作。
　　七、在遗址保护区内违法建设的，依照《城市规划法》、《文物保护法》等有关规定予以处理。破坏文物遗址的，由司法机关依法追究刑事责任。
　　八、本通告自颁布之日起施行。

一九九八年七月二十八日

1998 年 7 月 28 日，广州市人民政府发出《关于保护南越国宫署遗址的通告》，初步划定 4.8 万平方米的文物保护区，将遗址保护纳入广州市城市总体规划。

On July 28, 1998, Guangzhou municipal government released *Circular on the Conservation of the Palace Site of Nanyue state*, initially delimiting a cultural relics conservation area of 48,000 square meters and incorporating the site conservation into the city's master plan.

　　2009 年 5 月，《南越国宫署遗址保护性展示设计》经国家文物局审批同意。方案运用大遗址保护新理念，根据遗迹保存状况和可观性等，采取永久性回填保护或临时性回填保护，地面作标识展示或模拟展示，原址覆罩露明展示等方式对遗址进行保护和展示。

　　In May 2009, the *Design Proposal for Protective Exhibition of the Palace Site of Nanyue state* was approved by the State Bureau of Cultural Relics. According to the new concept of great site conservation suggested in the design proposal, permanent backfill protection or temporary backfill protection could be conducted in view of the preservation status and observability of the site, while the site could be protected and displayed through marking on ground or simulation and in-situ covering exposure exhibition.

2009年9月，由中国建筑设计研究院建筑历史研究所等编制的《南越国宫署遗址保护总体规划（2007-2025）》经国家文物局批准，并报广东省人民政府同意公布实施。

In September 2009, *the Master Plan for the Conservation of the Palace Site of Nanyue state (2007-2025)*, prepared by the Institute of Architectural History of China Architecture Design & Research Group, was approved by the State Bureau of Cultural Relics and presented to Guangdong provincial people's government for approval.

南越国宫署遗址保护范围：东至旧仓巷西边线，南至中山四路南侧的规划道路红线，西至昌兴街东边线一线，北至南越王宫博物馆用地范围北界及凌霄里。面积9.93公顷。

The conservation area of the Palace Site of Nanyue state extends east to the west border of Jiucang Alley, south to the boundary line of the planning road on the south side of zhongshan 4th Road, west to the East No. 1 Line of Changxing Street, and north to the north boundary of the Archaeological Site Museum of Nanyue Palace and Lingxiaoli, covering a land area of 9.93 hectares.

2008 年 10 月，南越王宫博物馆建筑设计方案竞赛委员会向社会公开征集南越王宫博物馆建筑设计方案，共有 12 个建筑设计方案参与竞赛，经过市民投票和专家论证，最终确定 6 号方案为建设方案。

In October 2008, the Committee of Architectural Design Competition of the Archaeological Site Museum of Nanyue Palace launched the design competition to solicit architectural design proposals. A total of 12 proposals were submitted, and No.6 Proposal was selected through public voting and expert evaluation.

南越王宫博物馆建筑设计方案（6 号方案）
Architectural Design Proposal for the Archaeological Site Museum of Nanyue Palace (No.6 Proposal)

修改完善后的南越王宫博物馆建设实施方案
View of Refined Design Proposal for the Archaeological Site Museum of Nanyue Palace

2009 年 8 月 29 日，南越王宫博物馆奠基建设
On August 29, 2009, the Archaeological Site Museum of Nanyue Palace broke the ground.

2010 年 4 月 8 日，南越王宫博物馆主体钢结构封顶
On April 8, 2010, the main steel structure of the Archaeological Site Museum of Nanyue Palace was topped out.

2014 年 5 月 1 日，南越王宫博物馆全面建成并对外开放
On May 1, 2014, the Archaeological Site Museum of Nanyue Palace was completed and opened to the public.

南越国曲流石渠遗址临时性保护回填施工现场
Temporary Protective Backfilling Scene of the Meandering Canal Ruins of Nanyue state

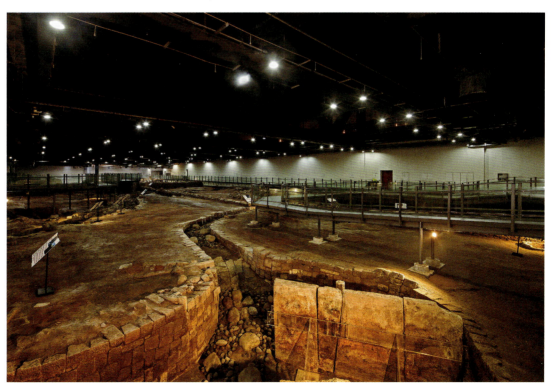

南越国曲流石渠原址露明展示现场
In-situ Display of the Exposed Meandering Canal Ruins of Nanyue state

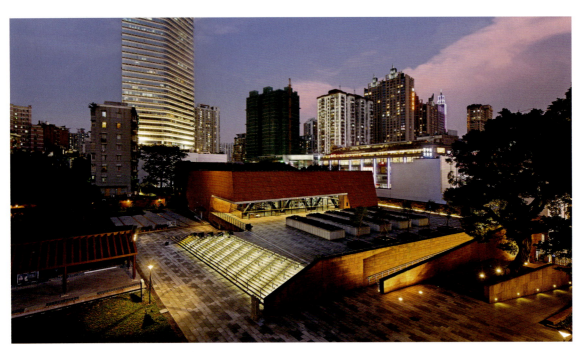

南越王宫博物馆曲流石渠保护主楼夜景
Night View of the Main Protection Building of the Meandering Canal in the
Archaeological Museum of Nanyue Palace

南越国一号廊道模拟展示
Simulation of No. 1 Nanyue state Gallery

海丝申遗

The Application for the World Cultural Heritage

南越国—南汉国宫署遗址是海上丝绸之路不同发展时期广州地区政治、经济、文化中心和海上贸易管理机构所在地，特别是南越国和南汉国两个政权的中枢所在，在南海海上贸易过程中扮演着重要角色，2016 年被列入"海上丝绸之路·中国史迹"首批申遗遗产点。通过申遗，开展主题价值研究、划定遗产区划、制定专项保护法规、进行本体保护和环境整治、宣传等工作，让宝贵的中华历史文化遗产更好地保护和传承下去。

The Palace Site of Nanyue and Nanhan states is the location of the political, economic and cultural center of Guangzhou and the Maritime Trade Administration in different historical periods, and especially the central governments of Nanyue and Nanhan states. It played an important role in maritime trade over the South Sea. In 2016, it was listed as one of the first sites of the Maritime Silk Road for World Cultural Heritage application. Through the application, it was planned to further conduct the theme and value researches, define the heritage conservation area, formulate special conservation regulations, conduct in-situ protection and environmental improvement, and promote the publicity, so that the precious historical and cultural heritage of China could be better preserved and passed on to the following generations.

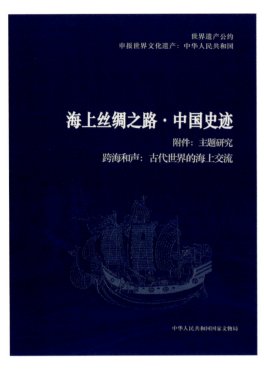

"海上丝绸之路 · 中国史迹"主题研究
Studies Themed on The Maritime Silk Road · Chinese Historical Sites

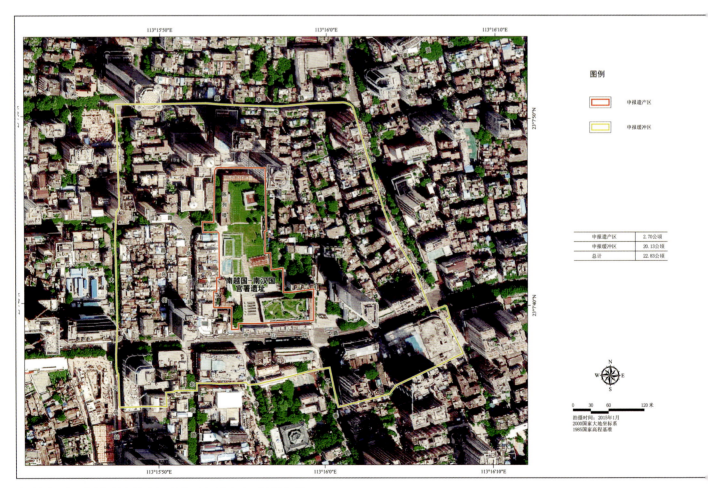

南越国—南汉国宫署遗址申报遗产区和缓冲区卫星影像图
Satellite Image Map of the World Cultural Heritage Application Area and Buffer Zone
of the Palace Site of Nanyue and Nanhan states

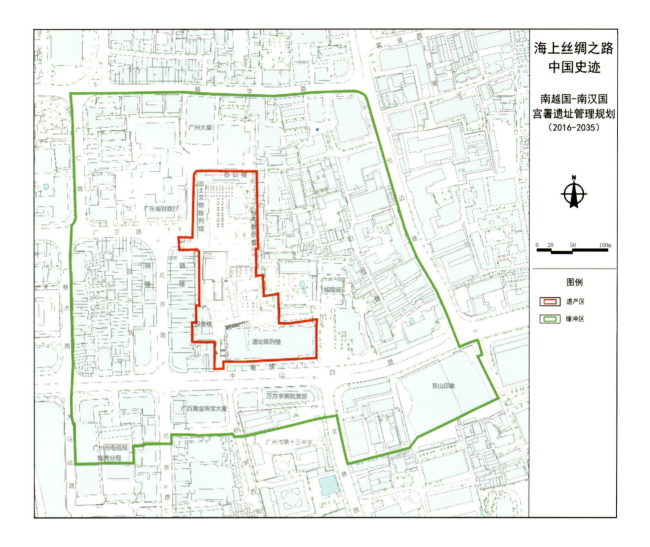

申遗范围地形图

南越国—南汉国宫署遗址遗产区四至范围以南越王宫博物馆（一期）围墙为界，面积 2.7 公顷。缓冲区东至仓边路西侧边线，南界至东山印象建筑南侧—广州市第十三中学操场北侧—广州市电信局越秀分局建筑南侧边线一带，西至广仁路道路西侧—广大路道路东侧—大马站路道路东侧边线一线，北至越华路南侧边线，面积 20.13 公顷。

Map of the World Cultural Heritage Acpplication Area

The world cultural heritage application area of the Palace Site of Nanyue and Nanhan states is of 2.7 hectares bounded by the walls of the Archaeological Site Museum of Nanyue Palace (Phase I) on four sides. For the buffer zone is in an area of 20.13 hectares, its east boundary extends to the west edge of Cangbian Road, its south boundary extends to the south of Dongshan Yinxiang Building, the north of the playground of Guangzhou No.13 Middle School and the south edge of the building of Guangzhou Telecom Bureau Yuexiu Branch, its west boundary extends to the west of Guangren Road, the east of Guangda Road , and the east edge of Damazhan Road, and its north boundary extends to the south of Yuehua Road.

南越国宫署遗址环境整治方案

方案包括外部环境和内部环境整治两大部分，其中内部环境整治由南越王宫博物馆负责，包括内部园林绿化提升、水井展示厅钢结构漆层翻新、博物馆红砂岩清洗、设备楼临时展览等。

The Environmental Improvement Plan for the Palace Site of Nanyue state

The plan includes two parts respectively for the external and internal environment. The internal environmental improvement is conducted by the Archaeological Site Museum of Nanyue Palace, including the internal landscaping improvement, the steel structure repainting of the ancient well exhibition hall, the cleaning of red sandstones, and the temporary exhibition of the equipment building, etc.

国家文物局关于海丝申遗史迹点南越国宫署遗址环境整治方案的批复
Official Reply of the State Bureau of Cultural Relics on Environmental Improvement Proposal for the Palace Site of Nanyue state, a Maritime Silk Road site applying for World Cultural Heritage.

园林绿化提升改造后的南越王宫博物馆
View of the Archaeological Site Museum of Nanyue Palace After Landscape Improvement

2016 年以来，为配合广州市海上丝绸之路申遗工作的顺利开展，提高市民对海上丝绸之路历史文明的认识，南越王宫博物馆多次组织广州海上丝绸之路专题展到省内外的社区、学校、博物馆等进行巡回展出，大力宣传海上丝绸之路的重要历史价值及世界文化遗产保护的相关知识。

To support the application work for world cultural heritage and improve the pubic understanding of the history and civilization of the Maritime Silk Road, the Archaeological Site Museum of Nanyue Palace has organized several exhibition tours on the Maritime Silk Road of Guangzhou since 2016. The exhibitions were presented at communities, schools and other museums of Guangdong Province and beyond, widely propagandizing the significant historical value of the Maritime Silk Road and relevant knowledge of world cultural heritage protection to the visitors.

2017 年"海阔羊城——广州与海上丝绸之路图片展"在德庆县博物馆展出
Vast Sea in yangcheng City: Photo exhibition of Guangzhou and the Maritime Silk Road was presented in the Museum of Deqing County in 2017.

2017 年 5 月 18 日，"南越国—南汉国宫署遗址与海上丝绸之路"专题陈列展在南越王宫博物馆开展
On May 18, 2017, The Special Exhibition of *the Palace Site of Nanyue and Nanhan States and the Maritime Silk Road* was presented in the Archaeological Site Museum of Nanyue Palace.

2018 年 "辽阔的南海——广州与海上丝绸之路文物展" 在云南红河州博物馆展出
Cultural relics exhibition titled *The Vast South China Sea : Guangzhou and the Maritime Silk Road* was presented in the Museum of Honghe Autonomous Prefecture, Yunnan Province.

附录：
南越国—南汉国宫署遗址大事记

1995 年　发现南越国大型石水池，遗迹原地保护。此次发现被评为 1995 年"全国十大考古新发现"之一。

1996 年　南越国宫署遗址被国务院公布为全国重点文物保护单位。

1997 年　发现南越国曲流石渠遗迹。经国家文物局专家组论证，认为南越国宫苑遗址是现存年代最早的中国宫苑实例。该发掘也被评为当年"全国十大考古新发现"之一。

1998 年　广州市政府发出《关于保护南越国宫署遗址的通告》。同年，广州市委批准成立南越王宫博物馆筹建处，负责遗址的日常保护和管理工作。

2000 年　在原儿童公园内试掘出南越国一号宫殿散水遗迹。广州市政府决定搬迁儿童公园，将地块交文物部门进行科学发掘和保护。

2002 年　自 2002 年开始，由中国社会科学院考古研究所、广州市文物考古研究所、南越王宫博物馆筹建处联合组成发掘队，对原儿童公园进行主动发掘。

2003 年　经广东省政府同意，广东省文化厅发出《关于公布全国重点文物保护单位南越国宫署遗址和沙面建筑群保护范围与建设控制地带的通知》，划定了南越国宫署遗址的保护范围和建设控制地带。

2006 年　由南越国宫署遗址等组成的南越国史迹被国家文物局列入"中国世界文化遗产预备名单"。

2007 年　6 月 9 日中国文化遗产日，中央电视台在广州南越国宫署遗址进行考古直播，向观众展示南越国遗迹的历史、文化价值和保护的重要性。

2008 年　中共广州市委、市政府决定依托南越国宫署遗址建设南越王宫博物馆。10 月，进行博物馆建筑设计方案竞赛，共 12 家设计单位提交了设计成果。

2009 年　8 月 27 日，南越王宫博物馆（一期）奠基建设。9 月 1 日，经广东省人民政府批复同意的《南越国宫署遗址保护总体规划》公布实施。

2011 年　世界历史遗址基金会将南越国宫署遗址列入"2012 年世界遗址观察名单"。

2012 年　由南越国宫署遗址等组成的海上丝绸之路史迹被国家文物局列入"中国世界文化遗产预备名单"。

2014 年　5 月 1 日，南越王宫博物馆全面建成并对外开放。

2016 年　南越国—南汉国宫署遗址被列入"海上丝绸之路·中国史迹"首批申遗遗产点名单。

Appendix:
Milestones of the Palace Site of Nanyue and Nanhan states

1995   The stone pond of Nanyue state was discovered and received in-situ protection. The discovery was named one of the top ten national archaeological discoveries in 1995.

1996   The Palace Site of Nanyue state was recognized by the State Council as the National Key Cultural Relics Protection Unit.

1997   Remains of the meandering canal were discovered. The expert team from the State Bureau of Cultural Relics commented that it was the earliest example among Chinese palaces discovered so far. The excavation was also named one of the top ten national archaeological discoveries of the year.

1998   Guangzhou municipal government issued the *Circular on the Conservation of the Palace Site of Nanyue state*. In the same year, Guangzhou municipal CPC committee approved the establishment of the preparatory office for the Archaeological Site Museum of Nanyue Palace, conducting the day-to-day protection and management of the site.

2000   Remains of the water apron of No.1 Palace of Nanyue state were unearthed in former Children's Park. Guangzhou municipal government decided to relocate the Park and hand over the site to cultural relics administration agencies for excavation and protection.

2002   From 2002, an excavation team jointly formed by the Institute of Archaeology, the Chinese Academy of Social Sciences, Guangzhou Municipal Institute of Archaeology and Cultural Relics and the preparatory office for the Archaeological Site Museum of Nanyue Palace started to excavate the site at the former Children's Park.

2003   Upon approval of Guangdong provincial government, the Department of Culture of Guangdong Province issued the *Notice on the Protection Area and the Construction of Control Zone of the National Key Cultural Relics Protection Unit of the Palace Site of Nanyue state and Shamian Building Complex*, defining the protection area and the construction of control zone of the Palace Site of Nanyue state.

2006   Historical sites of Nanyue State including the Palace Site of Nanyue state were enlisted in the World Heritage Tentative List of China by the State Bureaue of Cultural Relics.

2007   On June 9, China's Cultural Heritage Day, CCTV aired live show on the Palace Site of Nanyue state in Guangzhou to introduce the historical and cultural values of Nanyue state remains and the importance of protection.

2008   Guangzhou municipal CPC committee and municipal government decided to build the Archaeological Site Museum of Nanyue Palace based on the site. In October, a design competition was launched and 12 design firms submitted design proposals.

2009   On August 27, the Archaeological Site Museum of Nanyue Palace (phase Ⅰ) broke the ground.
On September 1, the *Master Plan for the Conservation of the Palace Site of Nanyue state* was issued and took force upon approval of Guangdong provincial people's government.

2011   The WMF (World Monuments Foundation) included the Palace Site of Nanyue state in the 2012 World Sites Watch list.

2012   Historical sites of the Maritime Silk Road including the Palace Site of Nanyue state were enlisted in the World Heritage Tentative List of China by the State Bureau of Cultural Relics.

2014   On May 1, the Archaeological Site Museum of Nanyue Palace was completed and opened to the public.

2016   The Palace Site of Nanyue and Nanhan states was enlisted as one of the first sites of the Maritime Silk Road for World Cultural Heritage applicatin.

后 记

　　广州古称番禺，是我国南海海上丝绸之路自秦汉时期形成，两千多年来持续发展、繁荣和变迁的重要港口城市，至今还保留大量与海上丝绸之路相关的文化史迹。为配合国家"一带一路"倡议的实施，2016 年，国家文物局根据国务院有关协调会议精神，决定推进海上丝绸之路史迹申报世界文化遗产工作，其中我市的南越国—南汉国宫署遗址等 6 处史迹点被列入首批海上丝绸之路申遗遗产点。根据申遗的工作任务和要求，需在各史迹点设立海上丝绸之路专题展览，充分挖掘各史迹点所承载的海上丝绸之路历史价值和人物故事，阐释史迹点与海上丝绸之路的关系。

　　"南越国—南汉国宫署遗址与海上丝绸之路"展览从 2016 年初开始筹备，同年 9 月，展览陈列方案初稿编写完成。10 月，根据我馆业务人员讨论意见，又对陈列内容进行调整和补充。11 月和 12 月，广州市海丝申遗办先后两次组织专家对方案进行评审，根据专家意见修改、完善后最终确定展览大纲。经过大家的共同努力，展览终于在 2017 年 5 月 18 日顺利开幕。

　　本展览得到中国文化遗产研究院和广州市海丝申遗办的高度重视和大力支持，广州市文化广电新闻出版局欧彩群副局长两次主持陈列方案专家评审会，并对展览工作落实提出指导意见；刘晓明总工程师亲自带领海上丝绸之路各处史迹点有关策展人员到南京、扬州等申遗成功的城市进行考察，学习、借鉴兄弟城市在举办申遗专题展览等方面的先进经验。此外，还得到陕西省考古研究院、广西壮族自治区博物馆、西安博物院、广州市文物考古研究院、泾阳县博物馆等单位的大力支持和帮助，为本展览提供图片、拓本等辅助展品资料。本书代序、后记的英文翻译由南开大学历史学院王音完成。在此，我们谨向所有参与、帮助、关心和支持本展览举办和本书出版的领导、专家、学者和同仁们表示衷心的感谢！

　　通过举办本展览，希望能让公众更多地了解南越国—南汉国宫署遗址与海上丝绸之路的关系，认识广州海上丝绸之路文化遗产，积极参与和支持海上丝绸之路的保护和申遗工作，把海上丝绸之路培育成国内外知名的文化遗产品牌，向世人全面、真实地展示古代中国与现代中国。

Epilogue

Guangzhou, known as Panyu in ancient times, is an important port city which witnesses the sustainable development, prosperity and transition of the Maritime Silk Road in the South China Sea for over two thousand years ever since Qin and Han Dynasties. Up to now, there still exist a lot of cultural and historical relics related to the Maritime Silk Road. To cooperate with the implementation of the national "the Belt and Road" initiative, in 2016, according to the spirit of the State Council's coordination meeting, the State Bureau of Cultural Relics decided to promote the application work of the Maritime Silk Road for the world cultural heritage. Among them, 6 historical sites of our city, including the Palace Site of Nanyue and Nanhan States, were included in the list of the first Maritime Silk Road heritage sites. According to the application task and requirements for the world cultural heritage, it is necessary to set up a special exhibition of the Maritime Silk Road at each historical site so as to fully excavate the historical value and character stories of the Maritime Silk Road carried by each site, as well as to explain the relationship between the historical sites and the Maritime Silk Road.

The exhibition of *the Palace Site of Nanyue and Nanhan States and the Maritime Silk Road* was prepared from the beginning of 2016. In September of the same year, the first draft of the exhibition plan was completed. In October, according to the discussion opinions given by the business staff of our museum, the exhibition content was modified and supplemented. In November and December, Guangzhou Municipal World Heritage Application Office of the Maritime Silk Road organized experts to review the scheme twice, and the exhibition outline was finally decided after modification and improvement according to experts' opinions. With the joint efforts of all, the exhibition finally opened successfully on May 18, 2017.

The exhibition is highly valued and strongly supported by Chinese Academy of Cultural Heritage and Guangzhou Leading Group Office of Conservation and World Heritage Nomination for Maritime Silk Road Heritage. Ou Caiqun, deputy director of Guangzhou Municipal Bureau of Culture, Radio, Television, Press and Publication, presided over the two expert review meetings of the exhibition scheme, and gave guidance on the implementation of the exhibition work. Liu Xiaoming, the chief engineer, led relevant curators of various historical sites of the Maritime Silk Road in person to cities like Nanjing and Yangzhou which had successfully applied for the world heritage to investigate, in order to learn from the advanced experience of brother cities in holding special exhibitions of applying for the world cultural heritage. In addition, this exhibition also received strong support and help from Shaanxi Provincial Institute of Archaeology, Museum of Guangxi Zhuang Autonomous Region, Xi'an Museum, Guangzhou Municipal Institute of Cultural Relics and Archaeology, Museum of Jingyang County and so on, which provided pictures, rubbings and other auxiliary exhibits for the exhibition. The preface and epilogue are translated by Wang Yin, lecturer of the Faculty of History, Nankai University.We here would like to express our heartfelt thanks to all the leaders, experts, scholars and colleagues who participated in, helped, cared for and supported the exhibition and the publication of this book!

By holding this exhibition, we hope to let the public know more about the relationship between the Palace Site of Nanyue and Nanhan States and the Maritime Silk Road, be familiar with the cultural heritage of the Maritime Silk Road in Guangzhou, as well as actively participate in and support the preservation of the Maritime Silk Road and the application for the world cultural heritage, for the purpose to cultivate the Maritime Silk Road into a well-known cultural heritage brand worldwide, and to comprehensively and truly show the ancient and modern China to the world.